CAESAR

A LEGAMUS TRANSITIONAL READER

TEACHER'S GUIDE

THE LEGAMUS READER SERIES

edited by
Kenneth F. Kitchell Jr., University of Massachusetts Amherst,
and Thomas J. Sienkewicz, Monmouth College

The *LEGAMUS* series was created to address the needs of today's students as they move from "made-up" Latin to the Latin of real authors who lived over two thousand years ago. Both established and innovative pedagogical techniques are employed to ease the problems facing students as they begin to read authentic Latin authors. At its core, the series intends to facilitate **reading** before all else, and the many innovations in the series all stem from a single question: "What makes reading this author difficult for students?"

The series is intended for use in intermediate and upper-level Latin courses in both college and high school. Volumes in the series may be used individually as an introduction to a given author or together to form an upper-division reading course.

Published

Vergil: A LEGAMUS Transitional Reader
THOMAS J. SIENKEWICZ & LEAANN A. OSBURN

Vergil: A LEGAMUS Transitional Reader: Teacher's Guide
LEAANN A. OSBURN & KAREN LEE SINGH

Catullus: A LEGAMUS Transitional Reader
KENNETH F. KITCHELL JR. & SEAN SMITH

Catullus: A LEGAMUS Transitional Reader: Teacher's Guide
SEAN SMITH

Ovid: A LEGAMUS Transitional Reader
CAROLINE PERKINS & DENISE DAVIS-HENRY

Ovid: A LEGAMUS Transitional Reader: Teacher's Guide
CAROLINE PERKINS & DENISE DAVIS-HENRY

Horace: A LEGAMUS Transitional Reader
RONNIE ANCONA & DAVID J. MURPHY

Horace: A LEGAMUS Transitional Reader: Teacher's Guide
DAVID J. MURPHY

Cicero: A LEGAMUS Transitional Reader
JUDITH L. SEBESTA & MARK HAYNES

Cicero: A LEGAMUS Transitional Reader: Teacher's Guide
JUDITH L. SEBESTA & MARK HAYNES

Caesar: A LEGAMUS Transitional Reader
ROSE WILLIAMS & HANS-FRIEDRICH MUELLER

Caesar: A LEGAMUS Transitional Reader: Teacher's Guide
ROSE WILLIAMS & HANS-FRIEDRICH MUELLER

CAESAR
A LEGAMUS TRANSITIONAL READER

TEACHER'S GUIDE

Rose Williams
& Hans-Friedrich Mueller

Bolchazy-Carducci Publishers, Inc.
Mundelein, Illinois USA

General Editor: Donald E. Sprague
Contributing Editor: Laurel Draper
Design & Layout: Adam Phillip Velez
Cover Illustration: Gheyn, Jacques de II (1565–1629): Julius Caesar Writing and Dictating to his Scribes at Ham House, London, Great Britain.
Photo Credit: National Trust Photo Library / Art Resource, NY

LEGAMUS Transitional Reader Series
Caesar: A LEGAMUS Transitional Reader
Teacher's Guide

Rose Williams and Hans-Friedrich Mueller

© 2013 Bolchazy-Carducci Publishers, Inc.
All rights reserved

Bolchazy-Carducci Publishers, Inc.
1570 Baskin Road
Mundelein, Illinois 60060
www.bolchazy.com

Printed in the United States of America
2013
by CreateSpace

ISBN 978-0-86516-736-0

CONTENTS

PREFACE:

The Purpose of This Teacher's Guide vii

INTRODUCTION:

Overview of Readings and Grammar Topics
Covered in Each Lesson ix

CAESAR AS GENERAL:
SELECTIONS FROM CAESAR'S *DĒ BELLŌ GALLICŌ*

Pre-Caesar Reading	Sallust *Bellum Catilīnae* 54	1
Lesson I	*Dē Bellō Gallicō* 1.1	3
Lesson II	*Dē Bellō Gallicō* 2.15.5–12	7
Lesson III	*Dē Bellō Gallicō* 2.20.1–9	13
Lesson IV	*Dē Bellō Gallicō* 2.22.1–5	17
Lesson V	*Dē Bellō Gallicō* 2.24.1–12	21
Lesson VI	*Dē Bellō Gallicō* 2.25.1–14	27
Lesson VII	*Dē Bellō Gallicō* 2.27.1–10	33
Lesson VIII	*Dē Bellō Gallicō* 2.35	37

CAESAR AS CULTURAL REPORTER:
MORE SELECTIONS FROM CAESAR'S *DĒ BELLŌ GALLICŌ*

Lesson IX	*Dē Bellō Gallicō* 6.13.4–7	41
Lesson X	*Dē Bellō Gallicō* 6.14.1–4	45
Lesson XI	*Dē Bellō Gallicō* 6.19.1–3	49
Lesson XII	*Dē Bellō Gallicō* 6.20.1–3	53

Lesson XIII	*Dē Bellō Gallicō* 6.21	57
Lesson XIV	*Dē Bellō Gallicō* 6.22	65
Lesson XV	*Dē Bellō Gallicō* 6.23	71
Lesson XVI	*Dē Bellō Gallicō* 6.24	77

CAESAR AGAINST THE SENATE: Selections from Caesar's *Dē Bellō Cīvīlī*

Lesson XVII	*Dē Bellō Cīvīlī* 1.1	81
Lesson XVIII	*Dē Bellō Cīvīlī* 1.2	87
Lesson XIX	*Dē Bellō Cīvīlī* 1.7	95
Lesson XX	*Dē Bellō Cīvīlī* 3.71	101
Lesson XXI	*Dē Bellō Cīvīlī* 3.72	109
Lesson XXII	*Dē Bellō Cīvīlī* 3.87	115
Lesson XXIII	*Dē Bellō Cīvīlī* 3.95	123
Lesson XXIV	*Dē Bellō Cīvīlī* 3.96	131
Conclusion & Post-Reading	Valerius Maximus *Facta et Dicta Memorābilia* 4.5.6	137
	Plutarch *Life of Caesar* 60–69	139

Appendices

The Undapted Latin Passages	141
Errata for the 2013 Student Text	169

PREFACE

The Purpose of this Teacher's Guide

The purpose and format of the *Legamus* series are fully explained in the "Foreword" and "Preface" of the student text *Caesar: A Legamus Transitional Reader* for which this Teacher's Guide has been written and therefore will not be repeated here.

The intention of this Teacher's Guide is to provide answers to the questions and exercises accompanying each Latin passage in the sections entitled "Now It's Your Turn," "Stopping for Some Practice," and "Thinking about How the Author Writes." For teachers' convenience, translations are also provided for all of the sentences in the exercises irrespective of whether students are asked in their text to translate the sentences or not. Additional information not required in the student answer but helpful for teachers to have at their fingertips is provided in parentheses. When questions are based on the unadapted Latin passage, "What Caesar Actually Wrote," where appropriate we provide line references based on the unadapted Latin passage line numbers not on those in the "Helping You to Read What Caesar Wrote" Latin passage. Answers to the questions in "Thinking about What You Read" are presented as suggestions and are by no means definitive or all-inclusive. This section endeavors to encourage students to think about their own reactions to Caesar's text and to make connections between today's world and the concepts raised in Caesar's narratives. Students will most likely give a variety of answers and the teacher will evaluate whether these responses reflect an accurate understanding of the Latin text in question. In addition, these answers should provide stimulus for class discussion.

As students build their Latin reading skills and their understanding of Caesar's writing, the questions in "Thinking about How the Author Writes" grow in complexity as do those in "Thinking about What You Read."

A copy of each Latin passage entitled "What Caesar Actually Wrote" from the student text is printed at the back of this Teacher's Guide. They are printed in the guide so that teachers can consult the Latin without having to look at the student text. The Latin in the guide is presented in a different layout so that teachers can use the passages for quizzes and tests for students. The translations are only intended to be one suggested translation of the passage. Gapped words are provided in roman font and brackets while alternative translations are in italics and brackets. The translations provide teachers an opportunity to check their own understanding of the text, as well as its grammar and syntax, or to assist students in improving their own translations.

Following this preface, the introduction provides an overview of each chapter's readings and grammar topics. Teachers can review this introductory material as they plan their syllabi for *Caesar: A Legamus Transitional Reader*.

Most of the lessons in the student text present the Latin arranged by sense units. We have also posted such arrangements of the Latin for lessons I, II, and IX–XII on the *Caesar: A LEGAMUS Transitional Reader* page on www.bolchazy.com.

We include a short list of errata in the 2013 printing of the student text. We appreciate students and teachers apprising us of errors.

Donald E. Sprague
Editor

INTRODUCTION

Overview of Readings and Grammar Topics Covered in Each Lesson

Editor's Note: Several topics introduced in the first lessons are again addressed in the later lessons where they receive a more intense discussion. The exercises accompanying the later lessons are accordingly more complex, requiring students to articulate the reasoning behind a given tense, mood, or the like.

Caesar as General in Gaul: Selections from Caesar's *Dē Bellō Gallicō*

Lessons I–VIII

Pre-Caesar Reading

Sallust *Bellum Catilīnae* 54
   Elliptical Writing
   Demonstrative Adjectives and Pronouns: *hic, haec, hoc* and *is, ea, id*

Lesson I

Caesar Discusses the Gauls *Dē Bellō Gallicō* 1.1
   Relative Pronoun *quī, quae, quod*
   Reflexive Pronoun *suī*

Lesson II

Caesar Encounters the Nervii *Dē Bellō Gallicō* 2.15.5–12
   Indirect Statement
   Adjectival and Adverbial Clauses: Relative Clause and *Cum* Clauses

Lesson III

The Battle Begins, Part 1 *Dē Bellō Gallicō* 2.20.1–9
   Verbals
   Infinitives
   Participles
   Passive Periphrastic
   Gerunds

Lesson IV

The Battle Begins, Part 2 *Dē Bellō Gallicō* 2.22.1–5
   Impersonal Constructions: *oportet*, *licet*, and *opus est*

Lesson V

The Thick of the Fight *Dē Bellō Gallicō* 2.24.1–12
   Pluperfect Tense

Lesson VI

Slowing the Onslaught *Dē Bellō Gallicō* 2.25.1–14
   Deponent Verbs

Lesson VII

The Hard-won Victory *Dē Bellō Gallicō* 2.27.1–10
   Result Clauses
   Purpose Clauses

Lesson VIII

The Outcome *Dē Bellō Gallicō* 2.35
   Deponent Verbs
   Impersonal Verbs

CAESAR AS CULTURAL REPORTER:
MORE SELECTIONS FROM CAESAR'S *DĒ BELLŌ GALLICŌ*

Lessons IX–XII

Lesson IX

The Druids of Gaul *Dē Bellō Gallicō* 6.13.4–7
   Conditional Clauses
   Indefinite Pronouns and Adjectives in Conditional Clauses

Lesson X

The Training of the Druids *Dē Bellō Gallicō* 6.14.1–4
   Cum Clauses Including Concessives
   Quod Causal Clauses
   Impersonal Verb with Substantive Clause

Lesson XI

Marriage among the Gauls *Dē Bellō Gallicō* 6.19.1–3
   Correlatives

Lesson XII

Politics among the Gauls *Dē Bellō Gallicō* 6.20.1–3
  Indirect Command

Lesson XIII

The Germans Live Simply *Dē Bellō Gallicō* 6.21
  Relative Clause of Characteristic (or Description)
  Dative with Intransitive Verbs
  Ablative with Special Deponents

Lesson XIV

Caesar Describes the German Lifestyle, Such as it May Have Been *Dē Bellō Gallicō* 6.22
  Purpose and Negative Purpose

Lesson XV

The Germans Do not Make Good Neighbors but They Do Treat Guests Well *Dē Bellō Gallicō* 6.23
  Indirect Statement
  Accusative Subjects of Infinitives
  Sequence of Tenses in Indirect Statement

Lesson XVI

Gauls and Germans Compared *Dē Bellō Gallicō* 6.24
  Ablatives Including Respect, Place Where, Manner, and Means

CAESAR AGAINST THE SENATE: SELECTIONS FROM CAESAR'S *DĒ BELLŌ CĪVĪLĪ*

Lessons XVII–XXIV

Lesson XVII

The Senate Debates Caesar *Dē Bellō Cīvīlī* 1.1
  Conditional Clauses

Lesson XVIII

Discussion, Debate, and a Decree against Caesar in the Senate *Dē Bellō Cīvīlī* 1.2
  Thinking about Time and Tense in the Indicative

Lesson XIX

Abused Tribunes and Insults to Caesar's Personal Dignity *Dē Bellō Cīvīlī* 1.7
  Genitive Review Including Possessive, Quality, Subjective, and Objective

Lesson XX

Pompey and Labienus Abuse Their Victory over Caesar *Dē Bellō Cīvīlī* 3.71
   Participles: Adjectives, Verbs, and Subordinate Clauses
   Participles Used as Adjectives
   Participles Used as the Equivalent of a Subordinate Clause

Lesson XXI

Pride before the Fall? The Pompeians Celebrate Their Victory *Dē Bellō Cīvīlī* 3.72
   Prepositions

Lesson XXII

Victory or Death: Labienus Insults Caesar and Swears an Oath *Dē Bellō Cīvīlī* 3.87
   Cum Causal with the Subjunctive
   Cum Temporal with the Subjunctive
   Cum Temporal with the Indicative

Lesson XXIII

Caesar Routs the Pompeians *Dē Bellō Cīvīlī* 3.95
   Guideposts: Uninflected Forms and Latin Syntax
   Adverbs
   Prepositions
   Conjunctions

Lesson XXIV

Caesar Visits Pompey's Camp, but Pompey Escapes *Dē Bellō Cīvīlī* 3.96
   Substantive Use of the Adjective

Conclusion & Post-Reading

Reflections on Caesar by Later Authors
Valerius Maximus *Facta et Dicta Memorābilia* (*Memorable Deeds and Sayings*) 4.5.6
Plutarch *Life of Caesar* 60–69

PRE-CAESAR READING

Sallust *Bellum Catilīnae* 54

What Sallust Actually Wrote (p. 4)

Translation

Therefore birth, age, eloquence were almost equal for them, greatness of mind [was] equal, likewise glory [was equal], but in other things they were otherwise [different]. Caesar was held [*considered*] great by [*on account of his*] kindnesses and generosity, Cato by [*on account of the*] integrity of [his] life. That one [i.e., Caesar] by gentleness and compassion was made famous, for this one [i.e., Cato] sternness added authority . . . In the one there was a refuge for the miserable, in the other there [was] destruction for the evil. The good nature of that one [*i.e., the former*], the firmness of this one [*i.e., the latter*] was praised.

After Reading What Sallust Wrote (p. 4)

1. In what qualities does Sallust find Caesar and Cato approximately equal?

    Sallust finds them approximately equal in terms of age, birth (i.e., social standing), and eloquence as well as greatness of spirit and glory.

2. Which man would be likely to inspire both respect and fear? Why?

    Cato would be likely to inspire both because he demonstrated integrity as well as severity toward wrongdoers.

3. Which man would be likely to be more popular? Why?

    Caesar is likely to be more popular because he is generous and merciful to the wretched.

LESSON I

CAESAR DISCUSSES THE GAULS

Dē Bellō Gallicō 1.1

Now It's Your Turn (p. 6)

Translate the following sentences, keeping in mind the grammar points mentioned above.

1. Caesar, quī nunc prōcōnsul est, dē Galliā scrībit.
   Caesar, who is now proconsul, writes about Gaul.
2. Flūmen Tiber est in Italiā; flūmen Garumna, in Galliā.
   The River Tiber is in Italy; the River Garonne [is] in Gaul.
3. Hī Gallī sē Celtās appellant.
   These Gauls call themselves Celts.
4. Hīs mercātōrēs saepe nōn veniunt.
   For these men [*them*] merchants do not come often.
5. Germānī, quōrum agrī trāns Rhēnum sunt, Belgīs proximī sunt.
   The Germans, whose fields [*lands*] are across the Rhine, are nearest to the Belgians.

Stopping for Some Practice (p. 9)

Choose the correct word to fill in the blank:

1. Gallī _____ (sē, eōs) Celtās appellant.
   sē; **The Gauls call themselves Celts.**
2. Belgae _____ (hās, haec, hōs) mercātōrēs non amant.
   hōs; **The Belgians do not like these [people].**
3. Germānī, _____ (quī, quae, quibus) fortissimī sunt, continenter bellum gerunt.
   quī; **The Germans, who are the bravest, constantly wage war.**

4. _____ (Ea, Is, Eōrum) flūmina sunt magna.

   Ea; **These rivers are large.**

5. Gallī linguīs inter _____ (eōs, sē, hōs) differunt.

   sē; **The Gauls differ among themselves in respect to languages.**

What Caesar Actually Wrote (p. 10)

Translation

Gaul is a whole divided into three parts, of which the Belgians inhabit one [part], the Aquitanians another [part], and [those] the third [part], who are called in their own language Celts, in our [language] Gauls. All these differ among themselves in language, institutions, and laws. The Garonne River divides the Gauls from the Aquitanians; the Marne and the Seine divide [them] from the Belgians.

Of all these the bravest [*most resolute*] are the Belgians, because they are farthest away from the culture and refinement of the Province, and least often merchants come to them and import those things that lead to the softening of spirits. They are next to the Germans, who live across the Rhine, with whom they are constantly waging war.

Thinking about How Caesar Writes (p. 10)

Translate this sentence in literal word order, then place it in standard English.

Gallōs ab Aquītānīs Garumna flūmen dīvidit.

> **The Gauls from the Aquitanians the Garumna River divides.**
>
> **The Garumna River divides the Gauls from the Aquitanians.**

After Reading What Caesar Wrote

Thinking about What You Read (p. 11)

1. In this passage Caesar sets out first of all to make the Romans understand the divisions between the Gauls. Why do you think understanding these divisions is important?

   The geographical divisions will make it hard for the Gauls to unite against an outsider. The cultural divisions will make them disinclined to do so or even to perceive the threat to a different group as a threat to themselves.

2. What does Caesar want the Romans to understand about the Belgians?

   Belgians are "tougher"—they are not likely to be hindered by humane considerations or complex thought, and they are accustomed to continual warfare.

3. What factors lead to their unique qualities among the Gauls?

   The first factor he names is their great distance from the civilizing influences of the Romans; the second is their proximity to the Germans, who are notorious fighters and with whom the Belgians regularly wage war.

4. What unfortunate effect does Caesar evidently believe civilization has upon "barbarians?"

   We can infer that Caesar believes it introduces them to luxuries and easier living. Love of these things lessens their desire to live and to fight in hard conditions.

5. How are modern feminists likely to view his expression of this belief? Please explain your view.

   Modern feminists are likely to take issues with Caesar as he seems to equate being feminine with being weak. Student responses to the second questions will vary—teachers should make sure students provide reasons for their view.

LESSON II

CAESAR ENCOUNTERS THE NERVII

Dē Bellō Gallicō 2.15.5–12

Now It's Your Turn (pp. 14–15)

Translate the following sentences as you keep in mind what you learned above. Any words not found in the Wordbank can be found in the glossary in the back of the text. Translate sentences containing indirect statements literally, then put them in more traditional English form. Translate the sentences containing clauses and identify the type of clause. See note above.

NB: Some sentences may contain both indirect statements and target clauses.

1. Belgae multī contrā populum Rōmānum coniūrāvērunt.

    Many Belgians conspired against the Roman people.

2. Caesar, quī in Prōvinciā erat, ad exercitum matūrandum sibi existimāvit.

    Caesar, who was in the Province, reckoned there should be a hastening to the army by himself.

    Caesar, who was in the Province, thought that he ought to hasten to the army.

    relative clause in the indicative, indirect statement, passive periphrastic within the indirect statement

3. Belgae, cum victī essent, Caesarī sē dedidērunt.

    The Belgians, after [*since*] they had been conquered, surrendered themselves to Caesar.

    cum clause in the subjunctive expressing cause

4. Helvetiī, cum pācem petīssent atque Caesar eōs in eō locō suum adventum exspectāre iussisset, pāruērunt.

    The Helvetians, after they had begged for a truce and Caesar had ordered them to await his arrival in this place, obeyed.

    cum clause in the subjunctive expressing circumstances

LESSON II

5. Dīviciācus clēmentiam Caesaris prō fratre suō petīvit.

   Diviciacus begged for Caesar's mercy on behalf of his brother.

Stopping for Some Practice (p. 17)

Choose the correct word to fill in the blank.

1. Caesar dīxit _____ (sē, eōs) hominēs esse ferōs.

   eōs; **Caesar said that they were savage men.**

2. Caesar sēsē petītiōnem Dīviciācī _____ (concēdere, concessit, concessūrum) et eōs in fidem receptūrum esse dīxit.

   concessūrum; **Caesar said that he was going to grant the request to Diviciacus and that he was going to accept their surrender [literally, "receive them into his trust"].**

3. Belgae quōs Caesar in dēditiōnem _____ (accēperit, accēpit) fortēs erant.

   accēpit; **The Belgians, whom Caesar received in surrender [i.e., whose surrender he accepted], were brave men.**

4. Caesar reperiēbat Nerviōs, quī Bellovacōrum fīnēs attigērunt, reliquōs Belgās _____ (increpitāre, increpuērunt, increpit).

   increpitāre; **Caesar discovered that the Nervii, who touched on the borders of the Bellovaci, were rebuking the other Belgians.**

5. Nerviī dīxērunt sē nullam condiciōnem pācis acceptūrōs _____ (esse, erant).

   esse; **The Nervii stated that they were going to accept no condition of peace [i.e., none of Caesar's conditions for a truce].**

WHAT CAESAR ACTUALLY WROTE (P. 18)

Translation

The Nervii bordered their lands. When Caesar inquired about the nature and customs of these, he learned as follows: that there was no approach to them for merchants; that they allowed no wine or other things pertaining to luxury to be brought in because they thought their spirits would be weakened [*relaxed*] and their courage diminished by these things; that they were fierce men of great courage; that they rebuked and blamed the other Belgians, who had surrendered themselves to the Roman people and cast away their country and their courage; that they insisted that they were neither going to send envoys nor accept any condition of peace.

After Reading What Caesar Wrote

Thinking about How Caesar Writes (p. 19)

1. Remembering that a Latin paragraph was like a long sentence, how does Caesar tie each of the first two sentences in this paragraph to the one preceding it?

   He uses a demonstrative pronoun in the first and a relative pronoun in the second; each has an antecedent in the preceding sentence. NB: Students might need to be reminded that an antecedent is the noun whose place the pronoun takes.

2. There are three stated and four implied uses of the pronoun *is ea id* in this passage. Find them and tell to whom each refers.

   The first *Eōrum* (line 1) refers to an antecedent in the sentence preceding this passage

   All these below refer to the Nervii

   ***eōs* (line 3)**

   ***eōs* implied subject of *patī* (line 3)**

   ***eōrum* (line 4)**

   ***eōs* implied subject of *esse* (line 5), *increpitāre atque incūsāre* (line 6), *cōnfīrmāre* (line 7)**

3. In this passage we find several types of infinitives used as verbs for indirect statements.

   Simple Present Active Infinitives
   esse increpitāre incūsāre cōnfīrmāre
   These are fairly straightforward; translate them literally.

   to be; to rebuke; to blame; to insist

   Present Passive Infinitives
   remittī īnferrī
   A present active infinitive performs action *mittere* "to send."
   A present passive infinitive, such as those above, receives action performed *mittī* "to be sent."
   Translate the two present passive infinitives above.

   to be relaxed/sent back

   to be brought in

Present Active Infinitive with Variation
relanguēscere
This one can be either "to weaken" or "to be weakened"
Explain which fits better in the passage above.

> **The passive, "to be weakened," works better as the Nervii are acted upon by the imports.**

Future Active Infinitives (with understood *esse*)
missūrōs acceptūrōs.
How do these two indicate purpose or intention?

> **The future tense of the participles connotes that the subjects are going to send and going to accept.**

Infinitive from deponent verb *patior*
patī
As we have said, passive forms of deponent verbs must be translated into the active voice.
Therefore, how is *patī* literally translated?

> **to allow**

Thinking about What You Read (p. 19)

1. What does Caesar want to find out before he advances into the land of the Nervii?

   He wishes to ascertain what their nature and customs may be.

2. Once again Caesar mentions the effect that foreign imports may have on native peoples. Compare his comments here to those in Lesson I. Cite the Latin.

   In Lesson I he gives his own opinion; here he says that the Nervii also believe that luxuries destroy courage (*Caesar cum quaereret, sīc reperiēbat ... quod hīs rēbus relanguēscere animōs eōrum et remittī virtūtem existimārent ...*).

3. What do the Nervii feel the rest of the Belgians have betrayed?

   They have betrayed their country and their courage.

4. How have they done this?

   They have betrayed their country by surrendering to the Romans.

5. What attitude do the Nervii have about the coming of the Romans?

   The Nervii have a negative attitude and thus they intend to send no envoys to the Romans and to accept no conditions of peace from them.

6. Discuss concerns a people might have when a foreign army comes into their lands.

> Foreign visitors, with or without an army, can bring new ideas and customs that may cause a people to question long-held communal values. Foreign visitors with an army may steal, pillage, or take over.

LESSON III

The Battle Begins, Part 1

Dē Bellō Gallicō 2.20.1–9

Now It's Your Turn (p. 23)

After identifying the participles or gerunds in the sentences below, translate the following sentences literally, rewriting them in standard English if necessary.

1. Caesar causā vexillī prōponendī prōcessit.

   prōponendī, gerund

   Caesar advanced for the purpose of displaying the flag.

2. Discere celeriter in proeliō necesse est.

   In battle it is necessary to learn swiftly.

3. Mīlitibus revocātīs, Caesar ad eōs prōcessit.

   revocātīs, (perfect passive) participle

   The soldiers having been recalled, **Caesar advanced to them.**

   After the soldiers were recalled, Caesar advanced to them.

4. Ex hībernīs iussū Caesaris discēdendum exīstimābant.

   discēdendum, gerundive (in a passive periphrastic)

   They reckoned that *there should be a departing* **from winter quarters** *by* **the command of Caesar.**

   They reckoned that they should depart from the winter camp in accordance with Caesar's order.

5. Discimus agendō.

   agendō, gerund

   We learn by doing.

Stopping for Some Practice (p. 28)

Choose the correct form to fill in the blank.

1. Caesar bellī _____ (gerere, gerendī, gessī) causā mīlitēs imperāverat.

    gerendī; Caesar trained the soldiers for the purpose of waging war.

2. _____ (Oppugnāre, Oppugnandum, Oppugnat) Nerviōs difficile erat.

    Oppugnāre; It was difficult to attack the Nervii.

3. Mīlitēs, aciē _____ (īnstrūctā, īnstrūxī, īnstruere) proelium gessērunt.

    īnstrūctā; The battle line having been drawn up, the soldiers waged war.

4. Discipulī in _____ (perdiscendī, perdiscendō, perdiscendum) memoriam remittunt.

    perdiscendō; The students relax their memory in learning (by heart).

5. Homō _____ (bellāns, bellandī, bellandus) cupidus erat.

    bellandī; The man was eager for waging war.

What Caesar Actually Wrote (p. 28)

Translation

By Caesar everything had to be done at the same time: the flag had to be raised, which was the signal when it was necessary to rush to arms; the soldiers had to be recalled from the works; those who had advanced a little further to seek [*for the sake of seeking*] ramparts had to be summoned; a battle line had to be constructed; the soldiers had to be encouraged; a trumpet signal had to be given. The brevity of time and the attack of the enemy was hindering a great part of these [*which*] things.

In these difficulties two things were [for] a help: the knowledge and experience of the soldiers, who, [having been] trained by earlier battles, were able to direct for themselves what might need to be done; and the fact that Caesar had forbidden legates to depart from the work and the individual legions unless the camp had been [*having been*] fortified.

These [soldiers] on account of the nearness and swiftness of the enemy no longer awaited the command of Caesar, but carried out on their own [*through themselves*] [the things] that seemed appropriate.

After Reading What Caesar Wrote

Thinking about How Caesar Writes (p. 29)

There are six adjectives and one perfect participle in this passage.

1. List them and discuss their use as describers.

    omnia (line 1) is used in place of the understood noun "things."

    ūnō (line 1) indicates that Caesar must multitask.

    magnam (line 5) shows how many of the activities are affected.

    duae (line 7) gives the number of positive factors.

    superiōribus (line 8) tells when.

    singulīs/singulōs (lines 9/10) indicates that no one must be alone.

    mūnītīs (line 10) (perfect passive participle) indicates what must be done to the camp before anyone leaves.

2. List the two adverbs that you find in this passage and tell how they are used.

    paulō (line 3) limits *longius* (line 3)

    longius (line 3) modifies *processerant* (line 4)

Thinking about What You Read (p. 29)

1. The passive periphrastic carries a great sense, not just of urgency, but of absolute necessity. These lines of the poet Catullus express the idea well:

    > *ūna salūs haec est. hoc est tibi pervincendum,*
    > *hoc faciās, sīve id nōn pote sīve pote.*
    > "this is the one safety. This has to be overcome by you;
    > this you must do, whether or not you are able."
    > Catullus 76.15–16

    Explain how this quote from Catullus connects to Caesar's narrative.

    The Catullus quote underscores the necessity expressed via passive periphrastic that one must do what needs to be done in order to survive. This parallels the set of "must do's," i.e., passive periphrastics that Caesar and his soldiers must accomplish to survive.

    NB: Teachers may point out to students that the passive periphrastic in line 1 colors the jussive subjunctive, making it a necessity as well. Students should be able to explain the parallelism of the *sīve* clauses.

2. There are seven passive periphrastics in the first sentence of this passage, six of which show specific activities. Which four of these express the usual Roman preparations for battle that now need to be done simultaneously?

   vexillum prōpōnendum (lines 1–2)

   aciēs īnstruenda (line 4)

   mīlitēs cohortandī (line 4)

   signum tubā dandum (lines 4–5)

Which two express extra preparations that must be made for this particular situation?

   omnia ūnō tempore erant agenda (line 1)

   ab opere revocandī mīlitēs (line 3)

3. Caesar is faced with a desperate need for multitasking. How does the second sentence further underline the perilous situation?

   The enemy is very near and is actually attacking.

4. In the second paragraph Caesar gives two factors that ultimately would go far toward saving the Roman army. What are these two factors? To which does Caesar give the most stress?

   These two factors are the long experience of the soldiers and Caesar's orders that they not scatter. He mentions the experience of the soldiers first, giving it major emphasis.

5. A major factor in an army's success is the ability of its soldiers to obey orders. How did the long training of Roman soldiers help in this emergency?

   Though trained to do what their commanders ordered, long experience enabled these soldiers to anticipate what those commands would be and act instinctually or out of habit even if Caesar had no time for official orders.

LESSON IV

The Battle Begins, Part 2

Dē Bellō Gallicō 2.22.1–5

Now It's Your Turn (p. 32)

Translate the sentences literally, changing them to standard English (as done in parentheses above) if necessary.

1. Subsidiō opus est.

   There is need for aid.

   Aid is needed.

2. Vexillum prōpōnere oportet.

   It is necessary to raise the banner.

3. Mīlitibus per sē ex castrīs discēdere licet.

   It is permitted to [*for*] the soldiers to depart from the camp on their own [*through themselves*].

   The soldiers are permitted to depart from the camp on their own.

4. Id facere mīlitī licet.

   This is permitted to [*for*] the soldier to do.

   The soldier is permitted to do this.

5. Hiemārī in Galliā oportet.

   It is necessary to [spend the] winter in Gaul.

   It is advisable to [spend the] winter in Gaul.

Stopping for Some Practice (p. 35)

Choose the correct form of the word.

1. Prōcessēbant magis ut tempus quam ut ratiō _____ (postulāre, postulābant, postulābat).

    postulābat; They advanced more as time than logic demanded. (They advanced more in accordance with the dictates of time than logic.)

2. Alius in Galliā, _____ (alia, aliā, alius) in Germaniā vīcit.

    alius; One conquered in Gaul, the other in Germany.

3. Nerviī Caesarem _____ (sequēbantur, sequēbant, sequēbatur)

    sequēbantur; The Nervii pursued Caesar.

4. Subsidium _____ (mitterent, mittēbat, mittī) poterat.

    mittī; Aid could be sent.

5. Saepēs _____ (prōspectus, prōspectum, prōspectū) impediēbant.

    prōspectum; Hedges blocked the view.

WHAT CAESAR ACTUALLY WROTE (P. 36)

Translation

The army was drawn up more as the nature of the place and the urgency of time demanded than as reason and order of military affairs [demanded], since different legions, some on one side and some on another, resisted the enemy, and the view was hindered by very dense hedges coming [*having come*] between. Neither was reliable aid [able] to be put in place nor was what in each part was needed [*there was need*] [able] to be provided, nor were all orders able to be managed by one [man]. Therefore in so great an adversity of affairs, various outcomes of fortune also followed.

THE BATTLE BEGINS, PART 2

AFTER READING WHAT CAESAR WROTE

Thinking about How Caesar Wrote (p. 37)

Add to each of the nominative nouns below the verb used with it in the passage and translate the statement. Tell the case and use of the other two substantives as they appear in the passage.

exercitus
  instructus est (line 1) the army was drawn up

legiōnēs
  resisterent (line 3) the legions resisted

hostibus
  (line 3) dative (object) after *resisterent* (line 3)

ūnō
  ablative of agent after *ab* (with *administrārī*, line 6)

Thinking about What You Read (p. 37)

1. How is this battle begun very differently from those to which the Romans are accustomed?

   The terrain, which the Romans had no chance to choose, is very difficult. The attack is sudden and the Romans had no chance to assemble into usual battle formation.

2. Why is it so difficult for the Romans to see how their fellow soldiers are faring?

   Dense hedges impede their view.

3. Generally fighting arms (wings) of the Roman army reinforce each other in difficulty. Why is this very hard to do in this battle?

   The battle is very sudden and the hedges impede both sight and movement.

4. Why does Caesar say that some parts of the army are doing much better than others?

   He says that circumstances are not equal for everyone. Not only are hedges thicker and the enemy fiercer and more numerous in some areas, but some have had the benefit of Caesar's presence and have had a bit more time to prepare.

5. How does that statement of Caesar's remove blame from the less successful? Is this a good military attitude? Please explain.

He makes it clear that the situation was much worse for some than for others. A good general, who wants to maintain self-confidence in his men, does not blame them for things that they cannot remedy.

LESSON V

THE THICK OF THE FIGHT

Dē Bellō Gallicō 2.24.1–12

BEFORE YOU READ WHAT CAESAR WROTE

Now It's Your Turn (pp. 39–40)

Identify the tense of each verb and translate the sentences.

1. Nostrī ab hostibus quī cesserant circumveniēbantur.

    cesserant—pluperfect; *circumveniēbantur*—imperfect

    Our [men] were [being] surrounded by the enemy [troops] who had given way [*yielded*].

2. Reliquī sē in castra recēpērunt unde erant ēgressī.

    recēpērunt—perfect; *erant ēgressī*—pluperfect

    The remaining [men] betook themselves [*retreated*] into the camp, whence [*from which place*] they had set out.

3. Quōs labōrantēs cōnspexerat, hīs subsidia submittēbat.

    cōnspexerat—pluperfect; *submittēbat*—imperfect

    He was sending reinforcements for those, whom he had seen [were] struggling.

4. Cum in eum locum unde erant ēgressī revertēbantur, tēla vītāre poterant.

    erant ēgressī—pluperfect; *revertēbantur*—imperfect; *poterant*—imperfect

    When they returned to that place whence [*from which*] they had set out, they were able to avoid the missiles [*spears*].

5. Hōs cālōnēs, cum cōnspexissent, subsecūtī sunt.

    cōnspexissent—pluperfect; *subsecūtī sunt*—perfect

    They followed these camp slaves after they had caught sight of them.

Stopping for Some Practice (p. 45)

Choose the correct word to go in the blank in each sentence.

1. Funditōrēs ūnā cum equitibus sē in castra _____ (recipiet, recipiēbant, recipisset).

   recipiēbant; The slingers betook themselves [*escaped*] into the camp together with the cavalry.

2. Cālōnēs praedandī causā ē castris _____ (ēgrediēbantur, ēgrediēbant, ēgressī).

   ēgrediēbantur; The camp slaves departed from the camp for the sake of plundering.

3. Clāmor eōrum _____ (quōs, quōrum, quī) cum impedīmentīs veniēbant oriēbātur.

   quī; The shouting arose [*became audible*] of those who came with the baggage.

4. Equitēs, quōs cīvitās Trēverōrum ad Caesarem auxiliī causā _____ (mittī, mittēbant, mīserat) ad castra vēnērunt.

   mīserat; The cavalry, whom the state of the Treveri had sent to Caesar for the sake of reinforcement, arrived.

5. Caesar eum trans Rhēnum in Germāniam mīsit ad eās cīvitātēs, quās superiōribus annīs _____ (pācāverat, pācāverant, pācāvit).

   pācāverat; Caesar sent him across the Rhine into Germany to those states, which he had pacified in previous years.

WHAT CAESAR ACTUALLY WROTE (P. 47)

Translation

At the same time, our cavalry and light-armed troops, who had been along with them—whom I had mentioned [were] driven back by the first attack of the enemy—as they were retreating into the camp, met the hostile enemy and sought flight again in another direction; and the camp slaves, who from the rear gate and the highest ridge of the hill had seen our men crossing [*to cross*] the river as victors, [and] having gone out for the purpose of looting, when they had looked back and had seen the enemy in our camp, they gave themselves to headlong flight. At the same time, the noise and shouting of those who were coming with the baggage arose, and they were borne some in one direction, some in another. Appalled [*Deeply moved*] by all these [*which*] things, the Treveri cavalry, whose reputation for [*of*] courage among the Gauls was outstanding, who had come, [*having been*] sent by their state for the sake of aid to Caesar, when they had seen our camp to be filled with the multitude of the enemy, the legions to be hard pressed and held almost surrounded, the camp slaves, cavalry, slingers and Numidians [having been] separated and scattered to flee in all directions, giving up hope of our affairs [*our affairs having been despaired of*] they returned home: They announced to their state that the Romans had been defeated and overcome and that the enemy had gained possession of their camp and their baggage [*the Romans (to have been) defeated and overcome, the enemy to have gotten possession of (their) camp and baggage*].

AFTER READING WHAT CAESAR WROTE

Thinking about How Caesar Writes (p. 48)

1. Caesar carefully structures his verb tenses:

    > levisque armātūrae pedites cum equitibus ūnā fuerant . . . occurrēbant
    > cum cālōnēs vīdissent . . . fugae sēsē mandābant
    > Trēverī vēnerant . . . vīdissent . . . domum contendērunt

    Noting the verbs, explain how Caesar builds a picture of cause and result or effect in each of the examples listed.

    > *Fuerant* is pluperfect. The light-armed troops had been with the cavalry and therefore were meeting the enemy along with them. Because the imperfect expresses continuous action in past time, *occurrebant* makes a clear distinction between what had gone before and what was happening at the moment.

    > In the second pair the same distinct relationship is shown between what the camp slaves had seen and their resultant flight.

    > The third pair shows what discouraged the Treveri cavalry and what they did about it. Their reaction is in the perfect tense. It is a completed act.

2. Perfect passive participles are among the strongest modifiers for nouns and pronouns, as they describe the subject in terms of what has happened to him. Find each of these perfect passive participles and match each with the noun or pronoun it modifies, then translate the phrase.

    > *pulsōs*

    >> *equitēs nostrī levisque armātūrae peditēs* our cavalry and light-armed troops having been driven back

    > *ēgressī (dep)*

    >> *cālōnēs* the camp slaves having gone out

    > *perterritī*

    >> *aliī(que)* others having been terrified

permōtī

equitēs Trēverī the Treveri cavalry having been appalled

missī

quī who having been sent

dissipātōs

cālōnēs, equitēs, funditōrēs, Numidās the camp slaves, cavalry, slingers, Numidians having been scattered

dēspērātīs

nostrīs rēbus our affairs having been despaired of

3. Caesar uses infinitives to build a graphic description of what the Treveri can see has already happened. It is hardly surprising that they are dismayed. Find these infinitives and translate them with the noun or pronoun they describe.

complērī

castra [nostra] our camp to be filled

premī

legiōnēs legions to be hard pressed

tenērī

legiōnēs legions to be held

fugere

cālōnēs, equitēs, funditōrēs, Numidās the camp slaves, cavalry, slingers, Numidians to flee

pulsōs (esse)

Rōmānōs to have been driven back/defeated

superātōs (esse)

Rōmānōs to have been overcome/conquered/defeated

potītōs (esse)

hostēs the enemy to have gained possession

THE THICK OF THE FIGHT 25

Thinking about What You Read (p. 49)

1. The brunt of a Roman battle was usually borne by the infantry, which had two major weapons, the sword and the spear. The legions were carefully divided into battle groups, each with its standard bearer around whom the soldiers rallied. The cavalry made the first sally, aided by light-armed auxiliaries, then fell back as the hand-to-hand combat began. Camp slaves worked in camp putting away baggage and getting ready to clean wounds and weapons at the end of the battle. If one part of the infantry was hard-pressed, the trumpet summoned another part to come up and fortify them. What was the first and major reason why this excellent plan never had a chance to begin?

    The soldiers were caught off guard while marching in and building their camp.

2. Because the Nervii broke through and pushed back the most hard-pressed of the legions, they managed to get into the Roman camp. Since auxiliaries were accustomed to think of the Roman camp as safely behind the lines, what effect did this have on the auxiliary troops?

    Since the auxiliaries were accustomed to thinking of the camp as a safe place behind the lines, seeing the enemy in the Roman camp dismayed them.

3. The Ninth and Tenth Legions managed to push back the Atrebates and get into the Gallic camp. How did this give a false signal to some of the Roman auxiliaries? What did they set out to do?

    Some of the auxiliaries took this as a sign that the Romans were winning; the hedges kept them from seeing that only two of the six legions were doing well. Thus they set out to loot, which was, to say the least, premature.

4. In the resulting chaos, what distant sounds raised even more fear among those fleeing?

    The sounds rising from the two Roman legions behind the baggage.

5. What does Caesar's dry comment about the Treveri cavalry *"quōrum inter Gallōs virtūtis opīniō est singulāris"* seem to indicate?

    That in this instance they did not live up to their reputation.

6. Why do the Treveri assume that all is lost?

    The Roman camp is filled with enemy, the legions are almost surrounded and hard-pressed, and the auxiliaries are fleeing in every direction.

7. Discuss this desperate situation in the light of Vergil's cryptic *Ūna salūs victīs nullam spērāre salūtem* "The only safety to the conquered (overwhelmed) is to give up hope for safety" (*Aeneid* 2.354).

   Again and again the Roman army and people showed a resolve in desperate situations that was their salvation. They did not give up until virtually every one of them was dead or out of commission. So Vergil, in his tribute to Roman history, is putting into the mouth of Aeneas a belief that made Rome outstanding.

LESSON VI

SLOWING THE ONSLAUGHT

Dē Bellō Gallicō 2.25.1–14

Now It's Your Turn (p. 52)

Translate the following sentences.

1. Calōnēs praedandī causā ad castra vēnērunt.

   The camp slaves came to the [enemy] camp for the sake of plundering.

2. Primipilus ad latus dextrum profectus est.

   The first centurion set out to the right side.

3. Centuriōnēs huius cohortis occīsī sunt.

   The centurions of this cohort were killed.

4. Signifer fortis interfectus est.

   The brave standard bearer was killed.

5. Mīlitēs gladiīs scutīsque usī sunt.

   The soldiers used their swords and shields.

Stopping for Some Practice (p. 57)

Choose the correct verb form to go in the blank in each sentence.

1. Legiōnēs ab hostibus _____ (pressērunt, pressit, pressī sunt).

   pressī sunt; **The legions were hard pressed by the enemy.**

2. Caesar mīlitēs vulnerātōs _____ (esse, sunt, erant) vīdit.

   esse; **Caesar saw that the soldiers had been wounded.**

3. Hostium aciēs ā dextrō cornū in fugam _____ (coniēcit, coniecta est, coniectae sunt).

   coniecta est; **The battle line of the enemy was thrown into flight by the right wing.**

4. Imperātor mīlitibus subsidium _____ (submittō, submittī, submittere) cupīverat.

   submittī; The general had wanted aid to be sent to the soldiers.

5. Centuriōnibus ā Caesare _____ (appellātīs, appellātō, appellandīs), spēs victōriae redintegrābātur.

   appellātīs; The centurions having been addressed by name by Caesar, the hope for victory was restored.

What Caesar Actually Wrote (p. 59)

Translation

Caesar set out from his encouragement of the tenth legion to the right wing of the army, where he saw his soldiers of the twelfth legion to be hard pressed and—the standards having been collected into one place—to be crowded together and to be a hindrance to themselves. All the centurions of the fourth cohort had been killed; the standard bearer having been killed, the standard had been lost; all the centurions of the rest of the cohorts either having been killed or wounded, among them first centurion P. Sextius Baculus, a very brave man, [who was] exhausted by many grave wounds, so that by that time he was not able to hold himself up. The others were slower, and some from the rear lines, their place in battle having been deserted, were withdrawing and avoiding weapons. He saw [that] the enemy [did] not cease coming up in the front from a lower place and [that they] threatened from every side and [that] the situation was in a narrow place and that there was no aid that was able to be brought up; a shield having been snatched from one of the soldiers in the rear, because he himself had come without a shield, he advanced into the first line, and the centurions having been called by name, having encouraged the rest he ordered the soldiers to bring forward the standards and spread out the maniples in order that they might be able to use swords more easily. The hope of the soldiers having been raised and their spirits renewed by his arrival, since each one in the sight of the commander even in his extreme [*last*] circumstances desired to perform energetically, the onslaught of the enemy was slowed a little.

After Reading What Caesar Wrote

Thinking about How Caesar Writes (p. 60)

1. Caesar's sentences are braided together like a rainbow of scarves. In the first sentence of this passage, the first clause states very simply that he went from one place to another, but his description of what he saw there is complicated, to say the least. He has explained it, as the poet Vergil sometimes does, from the perspective of the human eye as it takes in a panoramic scene. From the excerpts below, explain what Caesar first perceives as he views the chaos.

   suōs urgērī
   signīsque in ūnum locum collātīs
   mīlitēs sibi ipsōs ad pugnam esse impedīmentō

   > First he notices that the Romans are hard pressed, then he begins to perceive some of the reasons; namely, that the standards under which they fight have all been collected in one place, so that the soldiers themselves are a hindrance to their fighting.

2. In the second sentence Caesar takes in disastrous details, starting with the fourth cohort. Explain how these statements intensify the danger. Pay special attention to the military terms.

   First:
   Quartae cohortis omnēs centuriōnēs occīsī erant
   signum amissum erat

   Then:
   reliquārum cohortium omnēs ferē centuriōnēs aut vulnerātī aut occisī erant

   > The centurion, leader of one hundred men, was the immediate commander of his century. When he was missing, the chain of command broke down on the very first level of action. To make matters worse, the standard, around which soldiers grouped themselves before and after hand-to-hand combat, was lost, so this whole cohort had lost both of its primary sources of direction. The other cohorts of this legion are also missing commanders, and their standards are so crowded together that as a result the soldiers cannot group themselves effectively. The usual order and chain of command of a Roman legion is almost completely missing.

3. His gaze now goes to "the rest." Discuss the point Caesar is making with the use of the ominous words *"tardiōrēs," "excedēbant," "vītābant."*

   Not every Roman is a born hero; some have slowed their pace *"tardiōrēs,"* and are withdrawing from the action *"excedēbant"* or avoiding the action *"vītābant."* In other words, some of them have despaired of the effort and are just trying to save their skins.

4. The word *vīdit* in the penultimate sentence gives us more discouraging observations. What are they?

   The enemy is still pouring in on every side and there is no aid to be brought up.

5. Caesar's reactions are both physical and oral. Give the two verbs that show this.

   processit; iussit

Thinking about What You Read (p. 60)

1. Give two things Caesar notices immediately that are hampering the Twelfth Legion.

   Their standards are bunched and they are crowded together.

2. How bad is their situation?

   It is very serious, as they lack commanders to deal with the above situation or any other.

3. Caesar seldom mentions an individual. Why do you suppose he mentions Baculus by name? Please explain.

   This man is so gravely wounded that he cannot hold himself up, but the implication is that he is attempting to do so. He is not trying to get to the rear or to pretend to be dead. Thus, Caesar names him specifically, makes him an example, and places Baculus's story in immediate contrast to the deserters. Caesar sets him up as a true Roman patriot.

4. What does he find is happening among some of his weary soldiers?

   They are beginning to despair and sneak away.

5. What steps does he take to remedy this?

   He grabs a shield and begins to fight on the front line himself, encouraging the soldiers and then giving orders for spreading out both the standards and the soldiers.

6. What psychological factor helps the beleaguered Romans? Is this true of people in general? Please explain.

The fact that their chief commander is not giving up but is fighting among them as well as setting out tactics for improvement inspires the beleaguered Romans. Most people appreciate help from the upper ranks, especially if they bring both personal involvement and practical help.

7. Discuss some of the qualities Caesar possesses that make a successful leader.

Obviously he is brave. He possesses a horse, but makes no attempt to get away or even to stay in the rear. He is very observant and perceptive; he can see quickly where the trouble lies. He is quick of thought in supplying a remedy for at least part of the problem.

LESSON VII

The Hard-won Victory

Dē Bellō Gallicō 2.27.1–10

Before You Read What Caesar Wrote

Now It's Your Turn (p. 62)

Identify each of the following as purpose or result and then translate.

1. Nerviī tam fortēs erant ut Bellovacōs pellerent.

    result

    The Nervii were so strong that they drove off the Bellovaci.

2. Funditōrēs sē recēpērunt nē interficerentur.

    purpose

    The slingers retreated so that they might not be killed.

3. Impetus tantus erat ut nōn quisque superesset.

    result

    The attack was so great that not anyone [*no one*] survived.

4. Flūmen transīvērunt ut nostrōs occīderent.

    purpose

    They crossed the river so that they might kill our men.

5. Sabīnus clāriōre vōce locūtus est, ut magna pars mīlitum exaudīret.

    result or purpose

    Sabinus spoke with a rather loud voice in order that a large part of the soldiers might hear him. / Sabinus spoke with a rather loud voice with the result that a large part of the soldiers heard him. (Without context, it is difficult to decide.)

6. Mons altissimus impendēbat, ut facile perpaucī nostrōs prohibēre possent.

   result

   A very high mountain was in the way, with the result that a few men could easily block our men.

7. Tanta tempestās coorta est ut nūlla eārum nāvium cursum tenēre posset.

   result

   So great a storm arose that none of their ships was able to hold its course.

Stopping for Some Practice (p. 66)

For each of the following sentences, choose the correct verb, underline the *"ut"* clause, and label it purpose or result. Then translate.

1. Ad eum locum pervēnit tam opportūnō tempore, ut exercitus _____ (videātur, vidērētur, vīsus sit).

   vidērētur; result

   He came to this place at so advantageous a time that the army was seen.

2. Eādem nocte accidit ut _____ (est, sit, esset) lūna plēna.

   esset; result

   It happened the same night that the moon was full.

3. Fortissimus vir vulneribus cōnfectus est, ut iam pugnāre nōn _____ (potuerit, possit, posset).

   posset; result

   The very brave man was worn out by wounds with the result that no longer was he able to fight.

4. Hīs rēbus [i.e., angustīs fīnibus] fīēbat, ut Helvetiī minus lātē _____ (vagārentur, vagātī sint, vagentur).

   vagārentur; result

   On account of these things [i.e., their confined territory], it happened that the Helvetians ranged less widely.

5. Helvetiī frūmentum combūssērunt, ut domum reditiōnis spēs _____ (sublāta esset, subferrētur, subferrātur).

   subferrētur; purpose

   The Helvetians burned their grain, so that hope of a return home might be taken away.

What Caesar Actually Wrote (p. 67)

Translation

By the arrival of the tenth legion so great a change of the general situation [*affairs*] was made that our men, even those who lay back exhausted with wounds, leaning on [*having leaned on*] their shields renewed the fight; the camp slaves, having caught sight of the terrified enemy, even ran out unarmed against armed men; the cavalry also, so that they might by courage destroy the disgrace of flight, in every place by fighting outdid the legionary soldiers. But the enemy, even in the last hope of safety, exhibited such great courage that, when the first of them fell, those nearest stood upon those lying down and fought from their bodies; from these bodies thrown down and heaped up, those who survived threw weapons into our men, as if from a mound, and they threw back intercepted javelins: so that it ought to be judged that not in vain had men of such great courage dared to cross the widest river, to climb the highest cliffs, to undergo the most unequal position; which things the greatness of their spirits rendered easy out of difficult.

After Reading What Caesar Wrote

Thinking about How Caesar Writes (p. 68)

1. Comparative Adjectives

    As English adds "–er" and "–est" to make the regular comparative and superlative adjectives, Latin adds *"ior"* and *"issimus."*

    > slow, slower, slowest
    > *tardus, tardior, tardissimus*

    Latin comparative adjectives, declined in the third declension, have a masculine/feminine form *tardior* and a neuter form *tardius.*

    Latin superlative adjectives, declined in the first and second declensions, have the standard *–us –a –um* endings.

    A few third declension adjectives ending in *"–lis"* have the superlative ending *"–llimus."*

    Find the comparatives and superlatives in the previous passage. Please list them, and translate them.

    > *lātissimum* (line 11) widest, very wide
    >
    > *altissimās* (line 12) highest, very high
    >
    > *inīquissimum* (line 12) most unfavorable/disadvantageous
    >
    > *difficillimīs* (line 13) most/very difficult

2. Explain how Caesar uses comparison of adjectives to give his opinion of the Nervii.

   Caesar uses superlative adjectives to show both the difficulties the Nervii faced and the spirit in which they approached those difficulties.

Thinking about What You Read (p. 68)

1. How did the arrival of help affect the exhausted troops? Cite the Latin.

   Decimae legiōnis adventū tanta rērum commūtātiō est facta ut nostrī, etiam quī vulneribus confectī prōcubuissent, scūtīs innīxī proelium redintegrārent **(lines 1–3). (The key is that students cite the verb *redintegrārent*.) It encouraged them to renew the fight.**

2. What effect did it have on the auxiliaries who had fled?

   It encouraged them to show bravery to make up for their previous failures.

3. How did the Nervii react to the swift change in battle fortune?

   They fought harder.

4. What does Caesar have to say about this defeated enemy?

   He notes that their bravery and resourcefulness were incredible.

5. What does Caesar say should not be in vain?

   He says that such efforts should not go in vain.

6. After consulting the Sallust pre-Caesar reading and considering this passage, what do you think that Caesar's attitude is likely to be toward survivors?

   Caesar's famous clemency toward enemies is likely to be exercised toward the survivors, regardless of what they have cost the Romans.

LESSON VIII

The Outcome

Dē Bellō Gallicō 2.35

Now It's Your Turn (p. 70)

Translate the following sentences and label the verbs as regular active, regular passive, deponent, or impersonal.

1. Castra opportūnīs locīs erant posita.

    regular passive

    The camp had been pitched in an opportune place.

2. Impedimentīs castrīsque nostrī potitī sunt.

    deponent

    Our men got possession of the camp and baggage.

3. Accidit aestāte ut esset lūna plēna.

    Accidit **is impersonal;** *esset* **is regular active**

    It happened in summer that the moon was full.

4. Ad eum lēgātī revertuntur.

    deponent

    The legates return to him.

5. Legiōnēs in hīberna proficiscī iussit.

    iussit—**regular active;** *proficiscī*—**deponent**

    He ordered the legions to set out into winter quarters.

Stopping for Some Practice (p. 73)

Choose the correct verb for each sentence.

1. Caesar misericordiā in Nerviōs _____ (ūsa est, ūsus est, ūtuntur).

   ūsus est; **Caesar employed mercy toward the Nervii.**

2. Lēgātī ad Caesarem _____ (reversī sunt, revertēbāminī, reversī sint)

   reversī sunt; **The legates returned to Caesar.**

3. Mīlitēs multitūdinis adventū _____ (perterrēbant, perterritī erant, perterritōs esse).

   perterritī erant; **The soldiers had been scared by the arrival of the crowd.**

4. Litterae Caesaris ad Labiēnum _____ (perferre, perlātae sunt, pertulerit).

   perlātae sunt; **Caesar's letter was brought to Labienus.**

5. Germānī quī trans Rhenum _____ (incoluērunt, incolerent, incolēbant) ad Caesarem lēgātōs mīsērunt.

   incolēbant; **The Germans, who lived across the Rhine, sent envoys to Caesar.**

WHAT CAESAR ACTUALLY WROTE (P. 74)

Translation

By these things all Gaul was pacified. So great a report of this war was carried to the barbarians that from those nations who lived across the Rhine envoys were sent to Caesar, who promised that they were going to give hostages, and going to do his commands. Caesar, because he was hurrying to Italy and Illyricum, ordered these [*which*] envoys to return to him at the beginning of the next summer.

He himself, the legions having been led into winter quarters among [*in the land of*] the Carnutes, the Andes, [and] the Turones, which states were near to these places where he had waged the war, set out into Italy.

On account of these things [*revelations*] from the letters of Caesar, a thanksgiving of fifteen days was decreed, [a thing] which happened to no one before this time.

THE OUTCOME

AFTER READING WHAT CAESAR WROTE

Thinking about How Caesar Writes (p. 75)

1. The first sentence in this passage is stated in the passive. How does this make Caesar seem more objective?

   The ablative absolute (*Hīs rēbus gestīs*) followed by the passive (*Gallia omnis pācāta est*) does not explicitly mention the agent. Caesar is taking the position of reporter, not achiever.

2. What is the significance of *quae trans Rhenum incolerent*?

   These nations have a very formidable boundary between themselves and the Romans, yet they send messengers.

3. What does *quae* modify?

   nātiōnibus (line 2)

4. What does *quī* modify?

   lēgātī (line 3)

5. Who is the subject of the fourth sentence and how is that subject presented?

   The subject is *Ipse* (line 7)—Caesar refers to himself in the third person. Doing so lends the appearance of objectivity to his narrative.

Thinking about What You Read (p. 75)

1. In the first two sentences, how does Caesar stress the importance of the recent victories? What does he say has been achieved?

   He says that all Gaul was made peaceful by these affairs; he says that envoys were sent from several nations because these victories were considered so great.

2. What proof does he offer?

   Envoys from several nations, even those from across the Rhine, are coming to him.

3. Why is it important for Caesar to go to Illyricum? What is he stressing? (See Lesson I.)

   He is the governor of three important Roman strongholds there.

4. Caesar pictures himself as actively doing three things. What are they?

   Caesar's actions include giving a date for a return to the envoys, leading his troops into winter quarters, and setting out for his provinces.

5. What is the effect of Caesar's written reports?

   A thanksgiving of fifteen days is declared in Rome. This, Caesar says, is a tribute never given to any other honored person.

LESSON IX

THE DRUIDS OF GAUL

Dē Bellō Gallicō 6.13.4–7

Now It's Your Turn (pp. 78–79)

Identify the condition and translate the following sentences.

1. Nisi mīlitēs gladiōs habent, pugnāre nōn possunt.

   real (simple) present

   Unless the soldiers have swords, they are not able to fight.

2. Sī mīlitēs gladiōs habērent, pugnāre possent.

   real (simple) present

   If the soldiers have swords, they are able to fight.

3. Sī mīlitēs gladiōs habērent, pugnārent.

   unreal or contrary to fact present

   If the soldiers could [*might*] have swords, they could [*might*] fight.

4. Sī quis gladium habet, pugnāre potest.

   real (simple) present

   If someone has a sword, he can fight.

5. Nisi quis gladius habet, pugnāre nōn potest.

   real (simple) present

   Unless someone has a sword, he cannot fight.

Stopping for Some Practice (p. 81)

Choose the correct form of the verb.

1. Sī quis interdictus est, amīcī _____ (fugiunt, fugerent, fūgiant).

   fugiunt; **If someone has been outlawed, his friends flee.**

2. Nisi auxilium _____ (venīret, venit, vēnerīt), hostēs vincunt.

   venit; **Unless aid is arriving, the enemy is conquering.**

3. Sī auxilium venīret, nostrī _____ (vincerent, vincant, vincēbant).

   vincerent; **If aid were coming, our men would be conquering.**

4. Sī quid _____ (audiat, audiet, audit), id ad nōs dēferet.

   audiat; **If he should hear anything, he would report it to us.**

5. Nisi victor _____ (sit, est, fuisset), in castra nōn revertātur.

   sit; **Unless he should be the victor, he would not return to the camp.**

What Caesar Actually Wrote (p. 82)

Translation

These [Druids] attend [to] divine matters; they take care of public and private sacrifices; they interpret religion [*religious questions*]; to these comes a great number of youths for the sake of training; they are held in great honor among them. For generally about all controversies public and private they decide, and, if any crime is committed, if murder is done, if about heredity [or] about boundaries there is controversy, the same [ones] decide; they establish rewards and punishments; if any, either private citizen or people [*group/tribe*], does not stand [*abide*] by their decrees, they banish them from the sacrifices. This punishment is very serious among them. These so banished [*to whom it is so interdicted*] are reckoned in the number of the wicked and criminal; all depart from them, they flee their approach and conversation, so that nothing of contamination [*spread of disaster/trouble*] they may receive; neither is the right [of attending sacrifices] restored to them seeking [it] nor is any honor shared with them.

After Reading What Caesar Wrote

Thinking about How Caesar Writes (p. 83)

1. This discussion of Gallic customs differs from most of the sections we have read in that it does not include an action story or any individual traits. Note that there are no personal pronouns used. Find and list forms of the demonstrative pronoun *hic*. All but one of these forms refers to what two groups of people?

   Hōs (line 2): Druids; *hī* (line 4): Druids; *Haec* (line 8): refers to *poena* (line 8); *hī* (line 9): banished people; *hīs* (line 10): banished people; *hīs* (line 10): banished people

   They refer to the Druids and the banished people.

2. Discuss how impersonal pronouns are used in this passage both to avoid references to individuals and to show the scope of the activities mentioned.

> The first pronoun in this passage, *Illī*, differentiates the priests from the military knights discussed in the previous paragraph. After that various plural forms of the pronoun *hic* make the Druids a general group, "these," which brings them to the forefront, but only as a whole group rendering a common service or decision. Later the plural forms of *hic* form another general faceless group, the banished. Their punishment is lumped together with no indication of their individual characteristics or sins.

Thinking about What You Read (p. 83)

1. Caesar begins by listing three religious duties of the Druids. How do these duties give them great power over the minds of the people?

> They present religious services or matters, they carry out the sacrifices, and they answer any questions about religion. Since they present religious concepts, make the sacrifices that purify people and make them acceptable to the gods, and answer all religious questions, they can bend the attitudes of the people in whatever direction they choose.

2. What opportunity do the Druids have for perpetuating their power in the next generation?

> Because of their great power, many youth, probably the most ambitious and the brightest, come to them for training.

3. Discuss their double powers in both civil and criminal law.

> They are both judge and jury; they hear the cases, decide who is guilty, and render a judgment or punishment.

4. What recourse do they have if their decrees are not obeyed?

> As religious as well as civil leaders, they can prevent those who do not obey them from religious observances.

5. How powerful is this recourse? What are its ramifications?

> Evidently such banishment renders its recipient unfit for communication with his fellows. Thus he has no private or public life left to him.

6. Explore the likelihood of such a system being overthrown from within the society.

> There seems to be no effective way of rebelling against such a system without being cut off from one's fellows. As long as the people believe what the Druids teach them, they are not likely to rebel. Since the Druids get to train the brightest of the youth, leaders for a rebellion are likely to be lacking. The coming of an outside force, such as the Romans, is the most likely means for overthrowing such a system.

7. Discuss the role taken by religious leaders in the settling of the New World.

> NB: For this discussion, students can draw on their study of US history. The following points are by no means exhaustive.
>
> The Catholic monarchs of Spain, Isabella and Ferdinand, sent priests along on the voyage whose express mission was to plant the cross in these lands and spread Christianity. That objective is evidenced in Columbus naming the island on which he first made landfall *San Salvador*, "Saint Savior," a direct reference to Jesus Christ. The Pilgrims who founded the Massachusetts Bay Colony were a group of religious dissidents whose leaders exercised considerable power in the new colony. Lord Calvert founded Maryland, named for Mary, the mother of Jesus Christ, as a refuge for Roman Catholics who suffered discrimination in England. William Penn, a leading Quaker leader, founded Pennsylvania for his religious confreres. The religious leaders accompanying these groups of explorers, and then colonists, exerted considerable influence.

LESSON X

The Training of the Druids

Dē Bellō Gallicō 6.1.1–4

Now It's Your Turn (pp. 86–87)

Identify the subordinate clause in each and translate the following sentences.

1. Accidit ut Druidēs in Britanniā repertī sint.

   substantive clause

   It happened that Druids were found in Britain.

2. Caesarī cum id nūntiātum esset, mātūrat ab urbe proficiscī.

   cum **circumstantial or causal**

   When this had been reported to Caesar, he hastens to set out from the city.

3. Hoc cum vōce magnā dīxisset, sē ex nāvī prōiēcit.

   cum **circumstantial**

   After he had said this with a loud voice, he threw himself from the ship.

4. Hunc nuntium, cum ad eōs Caesaris mandāta dēferret, comprehenderant.

   cum **concessive [better: adversative]**

   They had arrested this messenger although he was bringing Caesar's orders to them.

5. Caesar questus est, quod, cum pācem ab sē petīssent, bellum sine causā intulissent.

   cum **concessive clause within a** *quod* **causal clause**

   Caesar complained because, although they had asked for a truce from him, they had waged war without (just) cause.

Stopping for Some Practice (pp. 89–90)

Choose the correct verb for each sentence.

1. Quod frūmentum in Galliā angustius _____ (prōvēnisset, prōvēnerat, prōvēnerit), Caesar coāctus est legiōnēs in plūrēs cīvitātēs distribuere.

   prōvēnerat; Because grain in Gaul had come forth (been produced) too meagerly, Caesar was compelled to distribute the legions among many states.

2. Cum ā prīmā lūce ad hōram octāvam _____ (pugnātum est, pugnārētur, pugnāvisset), nihil quod ipsīs esset indignum committēbant.

   pugnārētur; When (*during the entire time*) they were fighting from dawn to the eighth hour, they did nothing that was unworthy of themselves.

3. Accidit, ut ducēs adversāriōrum occāsiōne et beneficiō fortūnae ad nostrōs opprimendōs _____ (ūsī sunt, ūtantur, ūterentur).

   ūterentur; It happened that the leaders of our adversaries made use of the opportunity and benefit of fortune in order to overwhelm our men.

4. Labiēnus, cum captīvōs _____ (interrogāret, interrogāvisset, interrogāverit), omnēs interfēcit.

   interrogāvisset; After he had questioned the prisoners, Labienus killed them all.

5. Praetereā accidit, quod fierī necesse erat, ut mīlitēs ab signīs _____ (discessērunt, discessissent, discēderent).

   discēderent; Moreover it happened, as it had [*was necessary*] to happen, that soldiers were leaving their standards.

WHAT CAESAR ACTUALLY WROTE (P. 90)

Translation

The Druids are accustomed to be exempt from war, nor do they pay taxes along with the rest; they have freedom [*of*] from military affairs and immunity [*of*] from all situations [*circumstances*]. Excited by such great rewards, many come into the training of their own accord or are sent by parents and relatives. There they are said to learn a great number of verses. Therefore some remain in training for twenty years. And they do not think it right to entrust this knowledge [*these things*] to letters, although generally in other affairs, in public and private accounts, they use Greek letters. They seem to me to have established this for two reasons, because neither do they want the training to be brought to the common people, nor [do they want] those who learn, having relied on letters, to pay less attention to the memory: because it generally happens to many, that with the protection of letters they relax [their] diligence in learning and [their] memory.

After Reading What Caesar Wrote

Thinking about How Caesar Writes (p. 91)

1. Notice that *cōnsuērunt*, as noted above, is a shortened form of *cōnsuevērunt*. It is the only verb in the passage not in the present tense. Look carefully at the meaning of the word and explain why you believe Caesar used it.

    Caesar used this verb to indicate that this is something that happened long ago and, therefore, is now an established fact.

2. Caesar is now absorbed in presenting customs and he muses upon possible reasons for them. Discuss his use of impersonal verbs to signify his transition from factual reporting to speculation.

    He says, "they seem to me to have acted in this way for these purposes," and then gives a generalization about people's tendencies. He is careful not to give these statements as established fact.

Thinking about What You Read (p. 91)

1. How do the exemptions they enjoy make the power of the Druids even greater?

    They are neither killed in war nor impoverished by taxes, so their position is stable.

2. How do the exemptions give them an even greater hold on the future?

    These advantages draw the youth to them.

3. What is the great test of the mental acuity of the candidates for the order?

    The memorization of a great number of verses.

4. What two advantages does Caesar speculate that the Druids gain from their insistence on keeping their religious material unwritten?

    They keep religious knowledge strictly to themselves, and may manipulate it.

    They keep their memories sharp and have an excellent test of the mental abilities of candidates.

LESSON XI

Marriage among the Gauls

Dē Bellō Gallicō 6.19.1–3

Now It's Your Turn (p. 94)

Translate the following.

1. Collis tantum in lātitūdinem patēbat, quantum aciēs instructa tenēre poterat.

    The hill extended as far in width as the drawn-up battle line could hold.

2. Quantum mīlitēs castra protūlerant, tantō aberant ab aquā longius.

    They were farther away from water to the extent that the soldiers had moved the camp forward.

3. Cum omnēs eō locō convēnerant, tum nāvēs unum in locum coēgerant.

    Not only had everyone gathered in that place, but they had also brought the ships into one place.

4. Eō profectum est, quō nostrōs ventūrōs esse arbitrābātur.

    They set out [*there was a setting out*] for the place, where it was thought that our men would arrive.

Stopping for Some Practice (p. 97)

Choose the correct form of the word in parentheses.

1. Quantōs deōs habent, _____ (tanta, tantōs, tantum) sacrificia dant.

    tanta; **They offer as many sacrifices as they have gods.**

2. Eōs tantō spatiō secutī sunt, _____ (quantō, quantus, quantum) vīribus efficere potuērunt.

    quantō; **They chased them for as great a distance as they were able to accomplish in respect to their strength.**

3. Pompēius eō contendit, _____ (tantō, ibi, quō) Labiēnum
   mīserat.

   quō; Pompey hastened to that place where he had sent Labienus.

4. Helvetiī ibi ērunt, _____ (quandō, inde, ubī) eōs esse Caesar
   voluit.

   ubī; The Helvetians will be there where Caesar wanted them to be.

What Caesar Actually Wrote (p. 98)

Translation

Husbands, however much money from their wives as [*in the name of*] a dowry, so much from their own goods, an assessment having been made, they add to the dowry. Of all this money jointly an account is held, and the gains are saved; whichever of these survives in life [*outlives*] the other, to that one comes the share of both with the gains of earlier times. Men over wives, just as over children, have the power of life and death; and when the head of a family, [who was] born in the upper class, dies, his relatives come together and, if about the death anything comes into suspicion, concerning the wives they have an inquiry in the manner of slaves and, if anything is found, they kill the women, [*after they have been*] tortured with fire and all torments [*every manner of torture*].

After Reading What Caesar Wrote

Thinking about How Caesar Writes (p. 99)

Here we have two structures we have encountered before: the *cum* clause and the conditional clause. Both types of clauses may have either a subjunctive or an indicative verb. Locate the three clauses, identify the mood of the verb in each clause, and explain why the verb is in that mood.

> *cum paterfamiliae nātus dēcessit*—indicative because it simply gives "time when."
>
> *sī rēs in suspīciōnem vēnit*—indicative because it is a simple condition; it may or may not be true
>
> *sī compertum est*—indicative because it is a simple condition; it may or may not be true

Thinking about What You Read (p. 99)

1. What kind of gain does either partner in a marriage receive when one partner dies?

   The surviving partner receives both parts of the dowry and all the interest accrued.

2. How great are a husband's powers?

   He has the power of life and death over wives and children.

3. What great danger does a wife face when her husband dies?

   If his relatives are greedy and hope to inherit, they may seek to establish some guilt on her part for his death.

4. Discuss some of the opportunities for abuse of such a system.

   In addition to the possible interference of the surviving spouse's in-laws as noted in #3, a greedy spouse might well cause a spouse's death. A family member might insist on questioning the wife by torture and possibly having her executed for murder.

LESSON XII

Politics among the Gauls

Dē Bellō Gallicō 6.20.1–3

Now It's Your Turn (p. 101)

Translate the following. Identify the tense, mood, and voice of each verb of the subordinate clauses.

1. Nostrī cohortātī sunt inter sē, nē tantum dēdecus admitterētur.

    Our men encouraged each other, lest so great a disgrace be committed [*in order not to permit so great a disgrace*].

    imperfect subjunctive passive

2. Cīvitātī persuāsit ut dē fīnibus suīs cum omnibus cōpiīs exīrent.

    He persuaded the state to depart from its territory with all its forces [*that they should depart from their territories with all their forces.*].

    imperfect subjunctive active

3. Ambiorīx prōnūntiārī iubet, ut procul tēla coniciant.

    Ambiorix orders [it] to be announced that they should throw their spears from a distance.

    present subjunctive active

4. Comprehendunt utrumque ducem et ōrant, nē suā dissēnsiōne rem in summum perīculum dēdūcat.

    They embrace each commander and beg [him] that he not bring the situation into the greatest danger by means of his disagreement.

    present subjunctive active

Stopping for Some Practice (p. 103)

Choose the correct verb for this sentence.

1. Ut idem _____ (cōnātur, cōnārētur, cōnātus sit), persuāsit eī.

    cōnārētur; **He persuaded him to attempt** [*that he might attempt*] **the same thing.**

Translate these sentences.

2. Sī ex hībernīs fūgisset, hostium impetum sustinēre nōn posset.

    If he had fled from winter quarters, he would not have been able to withstand the attack of the enemy.

3. Sī trānsīre cōnārentur, Caesar eōs prohibēre posset.

    If they were attempting to cross, Caesar would not be able to block them.

4. Nisi subsidium submittētur, diūtius sustinēre nōn poterit.

    Unless aid is sent [*will be sent*], **they will not be able to endure any longer.**

What Caesar Actually Wrote (p. 104)

Translation

States that are thought to administer public affairs more advantageously have it established by laws, if anyone receives anything about the republic [*public affairs*] from his neighbors by rumor or report, that he report it to the magistrate and not discuss it with any other, because often it is thought [that] rash and unskilled men are terrified [*to be terrified*] by false rumors and urged to criminal acts and to take make decisions about the highest [*most important*] things. Magistrates conceal things that seem [best] and reveal to the multitude things that are of use. About public affairs except in the council it is not permitted to speak.

After Reading What Caesar Wrote

Thinking about How Caesar Writes (p. 105)

The first six lines of this passage make up one long sentence. There are two main clauses, joined by the conjunction *quod*.

1. Give the subject and verb of each of these two main clauses.

    cīvitātēs habent

    cōgnitum est

2. *Quae* (line 1) is the subject of a relative clause. What is its verb?

   exīstimantur

3. What are the subject and object of *accēperit*? This verb is found in what kind of clause?

   quis quid conditional

4. What are the subject(s) and verb(s) of the indirect command?

   quis dēferat nēve quis commūnicet

5. What are the subject(s) and verb(s) of the indirect statement depending upon *cōgnitum est*?

   hominēs terrērī et impellī et cōnsilium capere

6. What are the two verbs that go with *magistrātūs*?

   occultant, prōdunt

Thinking about What You Read (p. 105)

1. Notice that Caesar uses the word *commodius*, which means "more advantageously" or "more conveniently," to describe this facet of government. For whom is it more advantageous?

   It is more advantageous for the rulers.

2. Discuss the advantages and disadvantages of having rumors strictly controlled. Which of these did the United States founding fathers consider more important? How do these advantages and disadvantages impact our society?

   Student answers may vary. Some talking points follow.

   By controlling rumors, panics and revolutions may be avoided. However, the rumors may be true and may have great consequences. In such instances, the leadership might manipulate the information especially if it threatens their position. A significant disadvantage of controlling rumors is concentrating all power in the hands of the leaders alone. Recognizing such disadvantages, the founding fathers of the United States strove to place limits and checks on its leadership and thus they empowered the freedom of speech and of assembly, ensuring an independent press. In our society, because we enjoy a mostly unfettered press, informed citizens must beware the unsubstantiated story, look askance at the "news" in publications sold at checkout counters, recognize that the sound bite quote is often taken out of context, etc.

3. Discuss why political leadership might practice fact-concealment. Discuss also the ramifications of such concealed facts coming to light.

   Facts that might reveal weaknesses in the political structure or its failures will weaken the public's trust in that leadership. If such weakening continues, the political leaders may find themselves under siege or even stripped of power. Hence, political leadership practices fact-concealment.

LESSON XIII

The Germans Live Simply

Dē Bellō Gallicō 6.21

Now It's Your Turn (p. 108)

Relative clauses: characteristic or simple fact? Please decide, conjugate the verb in parentheses accordingly, and explain your choice. After you choose one, try the other, and explain that too! How does the meaning of the sentence change depending on your choice?

1. Caesar nullum mīlitum tribūnum habet, quī deīs immortālibus nōn _____ (fīdō).

    fīdat: present tense subjunctive, primary sequence; relative clause of characteristic.

    Caesar does not have a military tribune (literally, "tribune of soldiers") of the sort who does not believe in the immortal gods.

    This version describes the type of tribune Caesar employs in general.

    fīdit: present tense indicative; reports a fact.

    Caesar does not have a [single] military tribune who does not believe in the immortal gods.

    In the second version, we lay stress on the fact every single military tribune is god-fearing. There is not even one among them who is an atheist.

2. Germānī deōs habent, quōs oculīs suīs vidēre _____ (possum).

    possunt: present tense indicative; reports a fact.

    The Germans have gods that they can see with their own eyes.

    This sentence states facts. The Germans worship gods that they can see.

possint: present tense subjunctive, primary sequence; relative clause of characteristic.

The Germans have gods of the sort that they can see with their own eyes.

This version reports which of the various sorts of gods (visible versus invisible) that the Germans worship.

3. Gallia est omnis dīvīsa in partēs trēs, quārum ūnam _____ Belgae, aliam Aquītānī, (incolō) . . .

incolunt: present tense indicative; reports a fact.

Gaul is a geographical whole divided into three regions, one of which the Belgians inhabit, . . .

This version reports a fact. Belgians really do live in one of the three regions of Gaul.

incolant: present tense subjunctive, primary sequence; relative clause of characteristic.

Gaul is a geographical whole divided into three regions, one of which is the sort the Belgians inhabit, . . .

The second version implies that one region would be the type of area suitable for Belgians without telling us whether particular Belgians actually live there.

4. Tertiam quī ipsōrum linguā Celtae, nostrā Gallī _____. (appellō)

appellantur: present tense indicative; reports a fact.

The third region [those inhabit] who are called Celts in their own language and Gauls in ours.

This version reports a fact.

appellentur: present tense subjunctive, primary sequence; relative clause of characteristic.

The third region [those inhabit of the sort] who are called Celts in their own language and Gauls in ours.

This version is strange, as it occasions the question "what sort of people do these people call Celts in their language and the Romans Gauls in theirs?" The sentence would make much better sense if we were to substitute such adjectives as "intelligent," "savage," etc., as such words would imply a descriptive value judgment.

Verbs that do not take the accusative: supply the correct form of the word in parentheses.

1. Germānī _____ (agricultūra) nōn student.
   agricultūrae (dative singular)
   The Germans are not eager for [*do not take an interest in*] farming.

2. Germānī _____ (agricultūra) nōn fruuntur.
   agricultūrā (ablative singular)
   The Germans do not enjoy [*profit from*] farming.

3. Germānī _____ (Caesar) crēdunt.
   Caesarī (dative singular)
   The Germans do not believe Caesar.

4. Caesar _____ (Germānī) suādet.
   Germānīs (dative plural)
   Caesar persuades the Germans.

5. Licetne _____ (Caesar) _____ (urbs) potīrī?
   Caesarī (dative singular)
   urbe (ablative singular)
   Is it possible for [*permitted to*] Caesar to take possession of the town?

Stopping for Some Practice (p. 113)

Verbs that do not take the accusative: supply the correct form of the word in parentheses.

1. Druidēs _____ (rēs dīvīnae) praesunt.
   rēbus dīvīnīs (dative plural)
   The Druids are in charge of religious affairs [*divine matters*].

2. Caesar _____ (mīlitēs) nōn dēerit.
   mīlitibus (dative plural)
   Caesar will not fail [*be away from*] his soldiers.

3. Germānī _____ (castra nostra) potītī sunt.
   castrīs nostrīs (ablative plural)
   The Germans captured our camp.

4. Caesar _____ (victōria) fruitur.

   victōriā (ablative singular)

   Caesar enjoys [*experiences*] victory.

5. Nostrī _____ (hostēs) occurrēbant.

   hostibus (dative plural)

   Our men were encountering the enemy.

Relative clauses: characteristic or simple fact? Please decide, conjugate the verb in parentheses accordingly, and explain your choice. After you choose one, try the other, and explain that too! How does the meaning of the sentence change depending on your choice?

1. Hoc nōn est exercitus, quī Galliam Germāniamque _____ (dēvincō).

   dēvīcerit: perfect subjunctive, primary sequence, relative clause of characteristic.

   This is not the army of the sort that conquered Gaul and Germany.

   This better choice emphasizes the allegedly poor quality of the army that Caesar has with him. The indicative (*dēvīcit*) would simply state that Caesar did not bring one army (the one that conquered Gaul and Germany), but another.

2. Secūtae sunt tempestātēs quae nostrōs in castrīs _____ (contineō).

   continērent: imperfect subjunctive, secondary sequence, relative clause of characteristic.

   Storms ensued that kept our men in camp [i.e., such storms ensued that they kept, etc.].

   This example shows especially well how closely characteristic is connected to result. The indicative (*continēbant*) would fail to convey the character of the storms or the containment of Caesar's men as a result.

3. Hae cōpiae, quās vōs _____, ex dīlectibus in citeriōre Galliā sunt refectae (videō).

   vidētis: present indicative, statement of fact.

   These troops, whom you see, were recruited through levies in nearer Gaul.

   This better choice simply clarifies which troops are the subject of the sentence, i.e., the ones you are looking at. A relative clause of characteristic (with *videātis*) would not make sense in this context.

4. Deōrum numerō eōs sōlōs dūcunt, quōs _____ (cernō).

   cernunt: present indicative; these people really do perceive the beings that they consider gods.

   They reckon among the number of gods only those that they see [perceive].

   The version preferred by Caesar informs us that the Germans can see the gods that they worship. A subjunctive (*cernant*) would imply that there is a class of gods in general of the sort one can see.

What Caesar Actually Wrote (p. 114)

Translation

The Germans differ much from this custom. For they have neither Druid priests of the sort, who are in charge of religious matters, nor are they eager for [*do they engage in the practice of*] animal sacrifices. Among the number of the gods they consider those [gods] alone which they they perceive [with their senses] and by whose powers they are openly assisted: the sun and fire and the moon; the others [of the gods] they have not received [*heard of*] not even by means of rumor. All life [i.e., all their time] is placed in [*consists of*] hunts and in the practices of the military matters [*activities*]: from [the time when they are] children they are eager for [*the practice of*] effort and toughness. And those who have remained sexually inexperienced longest bear [i.e., receive] the greatest praise among them: by means of this thing [i.e., not having sex] some think that height and size are increased, others think that strength and muscles are increased. Indeed they think that to have had experience of a woman before the twentieth year [is] among the most foul things; of which thing [i.e., general awareness of the possibility of having sex] there is no cover-up [no pun intended; literally, *hiding*], because they both bathe in mixed groups ["promiscuously"; the English sense of the term derives from what can happen in mixed groups] and they make use of [as clothing] pelts or the small skins of reindeer, a large part of their body [remaining] nude.

After Reading What Caesar Wrote

Thinking about How Caesar Writes (p. 115)

1. In the passage you just read, identify all the verbs that take the dative, and explain why they do so.

   praesint: compound verb (line 2)

   student (x2): intransitive verb (lines 2, 7)

2. In the last sentence of the passage, why are *pellis, tegimentum,* and *corpus* in the ablative? Are they all in the ablative for the same reason?

   The words *pellis* and *tegimentum* are in the ablative with *fruor*. The word *corpus* is in an ablative absolute construction.

3. In the second sentence of the passage, *praesint* is in the subjunctive, but *student* is in the indicative. Can you explain why there is a difference in mood?

   The relative clause of characteristic (*praesint*) explains what sorts of priests the Germans do *not* have, whereas *student* reports facts. Germans love sacrifices.

4. One way to translate *Quī* at the beginning of the fifth sentence is as if it were equivalent to *et eī*. What is the grammatical term for this construction?

   Conjunctio relativa.

Thinking about What You Read (p. 115)

These questions are provided as an aid to sparking discussions. Responses can and should vary. Our answers are by no means exhaustive.

1. In this passage, Caesar is describing the sort of men his soldiers will have to face in battle. What do you suppose Caesar wants his readers to think about the Roman general and soldiers who will have to face such people?

   Because the Germans were so wild, fierce, and savage, the general and men who faced them must have been brave. Romans would have had cause to feel proud because Romans could face and beat such foes. They would also have respected Caesar for his skill and ability as a general because, again, the Germans were so different, so formidable, so frightening.

2. What factors contribute to a simple life? What is the minimum that people need to survive?

   Human beings require food, shelter, and clothing. What constitutes a minimum for some may not be nearly enough for others. Students will likely have a variety of opinions. Some may be attracted to the idea that they might be able to live off the land. Others might not be able to imagine a life without smartphones or hot showers.

3. What, if any, is the connection between lack of clothing and promiscuity? Why do you think Caesar was impressed that nakedness did not appear to promote promiscuity among the Germans? By way of comparison, what might Caesar's surprise tell us about dress in Rome?

> How much clothing people wear varies widely from society to society and from age to age. Romans, we can infer from this passage, wore clothing. The Germans frequently did not. That is why Caesar takes the time to describe it. The Germans were different. And because nakedness was a part of German culture, it was not considered sexually arousing. It was normal. A Roman outsider, however, might observe the nakedness of men and women in mixed groups as proof of the Germans' greater chastity, precisely because, in Roman culture, such nakedness would have been considered sexually provocative. By way of comparison, we may note, that in cultures where almost the whole body is covered, the exposure of almost any bit of the body can be viewed as something that might induce sexual arousal. An exposed ankle on an American beach similarly meant more in 1895 than it does today.

LESSON XIV

CAESAR DESCRIBES THE GERMAN LIFESTYLE, SUCH AS IT MAY HAVE BEEN...

Dē Bellō Gallicō 6.22

Now It's Your Turn (p. 118)

Use the verbs in parentheses in order to express purpose, and then translate each sentence. For good measure, identify the purpose as either positive or negative.

1. Germānī agrōs propriōs nōn habent, nē _____ (aedificō).

    aedificent: (present subjunctive, primary sequence) negative purpose.

    The Germans do not have their own fields, lest they build. That is, Germans do not own property in order to pervent themselves from constructing buildings.

2. Germānī impūberēs permansērunt, ut nervī vīrēsque _____ (confirmō).

    confirmārent: (imperfect subjunctive, secondary sequence) positive purpose.

    The Germans remained sexually inexperienced so that they might strengthen their muscles and strength.

3. Potentiōrēs humiliōrēs agrīs expellunt, ut fīnēs lātōs sibi _____ (parō).

    parent: (present subjunctive, primary sequence) positive purpose.

    The stronger [people] drive the weaker [people] from the fields, so that they may acquire wide territories for themselves.

4. Aedificō, ut frīgora _____ (vītō).

    vītem: (present subjunctive, primary sequence) positive purpose.

    I build so that I may avoid the cold.

5. Aedificāvī, ut aestūs _____ (vītō).

vītārem: (imperfect subjunctive, secondary sequence) positive purpose.

I built so that I might avoid the cold.

Stopping for Some Practice (p. 123)

Another way of looking at negative purpose is to express the concept as a fear clause. What one intends not to let happen is what one fears may take place. One fears "lest" (*nē*) it may happen. Positive purpose becomes the reverse. One fears that what one aims to bring about, and hopes will happen, may not. One fears "whether" (*ut*) it will happen, i.e., one fears that it may not happen.

Use the verbs in parentheses in order to express purpose or fear. Translate each sentence, and then state whether you have translated a purpose or fear clause. How are they similar? How do they differ?

1. Germānī agricultūrae nōn student, nē studium bellī gerendī agricultūrā _____ (commūtō).

    commutent: (present subjunctive, primary sequence) negative purpose.

    The Germans are not eager for [*do not practice*] farming, lest they exchange their zeal in waging war for farming.

2. Germānī timent, nē omnēs studium bellī gerendī agricultūrā _____ (commūtō).

    commutent: (present subjunctive, primary sequence) fear clause.

    The Germans are afraid that they may exchange [cf. lest they exchange] their zeal in waging war for farming.

3. Germānī opēs aequant, ut animī aequitāte _____ (contineō).

    contineant: (present subjunctive, primary sequence) positive purpose.

    The Germans make resources equal, so that they may restrain the common people by means of contentment of spirit.

4. Germānī timent, ut animī aequitāte plebem _____ (contineō).

    contineant: (present subjunctive, primary sequence) fear clause.

    The Germans are afraid that they may not restrain [cf. whether they may contain] the common people by means of contentment of spirit.

5. Marcus Calidius cēnsēbat, ut Pompēius in suās prōvinciās proficīscerētur, nē qua _____ (sum) armōrum causa.

   esset: (imperfect subjunctive, secondary sequence) negative purpose.

   Marcus Calidius proposed that Pompey should set out for his provinces so that there would be no reason for armed conflict [literally, of weapons].

6. Marcus Calidius cēnsēbat Caesarem timēre, nē ad ēius perīculum retinēre legiōnēs ad urbem Pompēius _____ (videō).

   vidērētur: (imperfect subjunctive, secondary sequence) fear clause.

   Marcus Calidius proposed that Caesar was afraid that Pompey appeared [cf. lest Pompey appeared] to keep his legions near the city as a threat to him [literally, "for his danger," i.e., Caesar's].

What Caesar Actually Wrote (p. 124)

Translation

They are not eager for farming, and a larger part [*the majority*] of their food consists of milk, cheese, meat. Nor does anyone possess a defined amount of land or his own boundaries [i.e., property]; but officials and leaders for individual years [i.e., for periods of one year at a time] assign to clans and the relatives of people, who have joined together [as a group], how much land and in what place it has seemed [best to them, i.e., the public officials] and in [one] year after another [i.e., every year] they compel [them, i.e., the people] to move. Of this practice [*thing*] they allege many causes: in order that, taken over [*captivated*] by a custom of being settled [literally, "settled custom"], they not exchange their zeal in waging war for farming; in order that they not be eager to acquire extensive lands, and the stronger expel the weaker from their holdings; in order that they not build more carefully for the purpose of avoiding cold and heat; in order that no [*lest any*] desire of money arise, from which thing partisan groups and arguments are born; in order that they restrain the common people by means of contentment of spirit, inasmuch as each may see his own resources [*wealth*] made equal with the most powerful [i.e., the wealth of the most powerful].

After Reading What Caesar Wrote

Thinking about How Caesar Writes (p. 125)

1. In the passage you just read, find all the purpose clauses.

    nē adsiduā consuētūdine captī studium bellī gerendī agricultūrā commūtent (lines 6–7)

    nē lātōs fīnēs parāre studeant, potentiōrēsque humiliōrēs possessiōnibus expellant (lines 8–9)

    nē accūrātius ad frīgora atque aestūs vītandōs aedificent (lines 9–10)

    nē qua oriātur pecūniae cupiditās (line 10)

    ut animī aequitāte plebem contineant (lines 11–12)

2. In the passage you just read, there is one clause that expresses purpose without using the subjunctive. Please find this clause, and identify the construction.

    Ēius reī multās adferunt causās (line 6): *causa* plus the genitive routinely expresses purpose, although the question is really not entirely fair here, as the construction that expresses purpose uses *causā* in the ablative plus a gerund or gerundive construction in the genitive. On the other hand, "the many reasons for this practice" also serve to introduce the string of purpose clauses that follow, so we thought the question might be worth posing!

3. There is a clause in the passage you just read that uses the subjunctive, but does not express purpose. Please find this clause, and explain why this clause uses the subjunctive.

    cum suās quisque opēs cum potentissimīs aequārī videat (line 12): *cum* clause because it is expressing cause.

4. The verb *nascuntur* is in the indicative mood, even though it appears in a subordinate clause dependent on another clause in the subjunctive. What does the indicative mood express here rather dramatically (at least after you think about it)?

    By using the indicative, Caesar states rather dramatically this is a well-established fact.

Thinking about What You Read (p. 125)

These questions are provided as an aid to sparking discussions. Responses can and should vary. Our answers are by no means exhaustive.

1. Much of the world is edible, but different peoples tend to eat just a small subset of what could actually provide nutrition. Does it matter what people eat, so long as they obtain enough, but not too many calories? Why?

   Insects are incredibly nutritious, ubiquitous, and easy to raise, and they do not serve as hosts for dangerous viruses that can jump from their species to ours. And yet most would find this potential source of food revolting. Similarly, North Americans shun cats, dogs, and horses, but consider such equally intelligent and sentient mammals as cows and pigs fair game. What we are willing to eat tells us about who we are. Caesar was obviously aware of this. His audience would have found German eating habits interesting for what it told them about how different the Germans were from Romans.

2. In defining ethnic identity, do you think that the kinds of food people eat matter as much as what language they speak? Please explain.

   One might illustrate the point by first naming languages, asking students to identify cultures associated with the language. One could then use foods to separate cultures that share languages. For example, language: English; three cultures: British, American (United States), Australian; foods: kippers (British); hotdogs (American); vegemite (Australian).

3. How do property rights affect where we live, build, and grow our food?

   If we do not own or somehow control a specific property, we are unlikely to invest the time and effort it takes to grow a crop. Agriculture is only possible when groups and individuals can be sure of controlling land long enough to plant, care for, and harvest a crop.

4. When Caesar writes about the lower classes, upper classes, the weak, the powerful, and their conflicts or social harmony, we must always remember that he writes for a Roman audience that relatively recently had lived through a civil war and that was on the verge of another. What do you think Caesar tries to convey to his Roman audience about the sources of social unrest and class conflict?

   When the lower classes are indebted to the ruling class and lack opportunities to repay their debts or thrive economically, they grow to resent the ruling class, and, if their unhappiness becomes widespread, they may even revolt, which can lead to indiscriminate violence against all classes. Moreover, political opportunists, both upper and lower class, can exploit economic and political dissatisfaction to build their own power, creating factions and further instability. Debt was a problem in ancient Rome. Landless citizens with little opportunity for economic advancement represented another. They had trouble competing with slave labor. And indebted individuals in Rome could see the wealth of the ruling classes on frequent display, leading to further resentments—and ambitions, often thwarted. Germans, on the other hand, avoided (in Caesar's portrait) such problems by keeping everyone at the same subsistence level. Germans were poor, but tough, and united. But please keep in mind that Caesar's view is idealized!

LESSON XV

THE GERMANS DO NOT MAKE GOOD NEIGHBORS BUT THEY DO TREAT GUESTS WELL

Dē Bellō Gallicō 6.23

Now It's Your Turn (p. 129)

Adjust your translation as necessary. How and why does your translation change? How does the tense of the main verb affect your translation in English of the same infinitive?

> Students should note that the verb of the indirect statement is translated differently based on whether the main verb is primary or secondary.

1. *Dīxit sē ducem fore.*   He said that he _____ the leader.
   would be
   future infinitive in secondary sequence

2. *Dīcit sē ducem fore.*   He says that he _____ the leader.
   will be
   future infinitive in primary sequence

3. *Dīxit sē ducem esse.*   He said that he _____ the leader.
   was
   present infinitive in secondary sequence

4. *Dīcit sē ducem esse.*   He says that he _____ the leader.
   is
   present infinitive in primary sequence

5. *Dīxit sē ducem fuisse.*   He said that he _____ the leader.
   had been
   perfect infinitive in secondary sequence

6. *Dīcit sē ducem fuisse.* He says that he _____ the leader.

   was

   perfect infintive in primary sequence

Stopping for Some Practice (pp. 133–134)

Translate each pair of sentences. How and why does your translation change? How does the tense of the main verb affect your translation in English of the same infinitive?

> Students should note that the verb of the indirect statement is translated differently based on whether the main verb is primary or secondary.

1. Hoc esse proprium virtūtis Germānī existimant.
2. Hoc esse proprium virtūtis Germānī existimāvērunt.

   They *reckon* that this *is* an element of manliness.

   They *reckoned* that this *was* an element of manliness.

3. Germānī sē fore tūtiōrēs arbitrantur.
4. Germānī sē fore tūtiōrēs arbitrātī sunt.

   The Germans *think* that they *will be* safer.

   The Germans *thought* that they *would be* safer.

5. Nōn illī paucitātem nostrōrum mīlitum causae fuisse cōgitant.
6. Nōn illī paucitātem nostrōrum mīlitum causae fuisse cōgitābant.

   They *do* not *consider* [the possibility] that the fewness of our soldiers *was* a cause.

   They *did* not *consider* [the possibility] that the fewness of our soldiers *had been* a cause.

   NB: *causae*: "for a cause," i.e., the reason for something, in this case, a defeat; dative of purpose.

What Caesar Actually Wrote (p. 135)

Translation

For the states [*tribes*] the greatest praise is to have deserted territories—their boundaries having been laid waste—as widely as possible round about themselves. They reckon that this thing [is] an element of manliness, that neighbors expelled from their lands yield, and that no one dares to settle nearby; at the same time by means of this thing they think that they will be safer—the fear of sudden invasion having been removed. Whenever a state wages [aggressive] war or defends against war brought in [i.e., an invasion], they choose magistrates who are to be in charge of that war, so that they may have the power of life and death [i.e., absolute authority]. In peace there is no common magistrate, but leaders of the regions and districts administer justice among their people and settle disputes. Highway robberies have no ill fame, which beyond the borders of the state are committed, and they claim that these are committed for the sake of training the youth and diminishing inactivity. And when someone among the leaders in an assembly has said that he will be a leader, [those] who may wish to follow should make a declaration. Those who approve the purpose and the man arise, and they promise their aid and by the crowd they are praised: and those who of these have not followed are reckoned among the number of deserters and traitors, and afterward credibility in all matters is taken away from them. They do not consider it religiously permissible to violate [the rights and obligations of] hospitality; [those] who have come to them for whatever reason, they keep from [suffering] wrongdoing, they consider them sacred [i.e., inviolable], and to them the houses of all men are open and food is shared.

AFTER READING WHAT CAESAR WROTE

Thinking about How Caesar Writes (p. 136)

1. In the passage you just read, identify all accusative subjects and the infinitives for which they are the subjects.

   fīnitimōs cēdere (line 3)

   quemquam audēre consistere (lines 3–4)

   sē fore (line 4)

   ea fīerī (lines 10–11)

   sē fore (line 12)

   fās [*esse*] *violāre* (line 17)

   [*eōs*] *sanctōs* [*esse*] (line 18)

2. Of those subjects and infinitives you identified in number one, how many of them are in indirect statement? Can you find an example of an accusative subject of an infinitive that is in some other sort of construction? Please identify that instance and its construction.

   > All of the examples are in indirect statement. When we wrote the question, we erroneously thought that there was an instance of an accusative subject of an infinitive that was not in indirect statement. It is certainly worth looking for such constructions. Alas, we do not find an example in this passage.

3. Can you find a relative clause of characteristic and a use of the gerundive to express purpose in this passage?

Relative clause of characteristic: *quī eī bellō praesint* (line 6)

Gerundive construction: *iuventūtis exercendae ac dēsidiae minuendae causā* (lines 10–11)

Thinking about What You Read (p. 136)

These questions are provided as an aid to sparking discussions. Responses can and should vary. Our answers are by no means exhaustive.

1. Some people do not like to have neighbors living close by. Why? Robert Frost famously wrote that "good fences make good neighbors." Do you agree? Why or why not?

   Neighbors can be loud, encroach on one's property, or steal one's crops and possessions. Not all neighbors are good. Living far away can spare one the irritations of having to deal with such annoyances or dangers. Fences, and clear property lines, help settle disputes before they even begin. Who owns what is clear.

2. Why are near neighbors potential problems for states, countries, nations, and people?

   The problems that people encounter on a small scale are not dissimilar to those that occur on a large scale. Neighboring states may want to take wealth, resources, and territory for themselves.

3. In the ancient world, hospitality (offering food and shelter to travelers) was often considered a religious obligation. What factors do you think contributed to such an odd (from the modern point of view) concept?

   Travel in the ancient world was difficult. Well-developed systems of hotels and restaurants did not exist. Hospitality, especially in less developed areas, helped compensate for this lack of basic amenities. Nevertheless, travel remained dangerous.

4. The Germans, according to Caesar, observe rules and laws, both human and religious, but those regulations extend only to their own group. What is the consequence of treating people outside their group as not subject to the same rules? Can you think of any other examples? Why is this problematic?

   The Germans are free to treat non-Germans as not fully human. They are free to steal from them and treat them as enemies. Romans similarly did not respect non-Romans as deserving the protections enjoyed by Roman citizens. And the United States today makes distinctions between US citizens and non-citizens (constitutional protections extended to US citizens are frequently not extended to non-citizens, especially outside the borders of the United States). Despite the United Nations, and various efforts to establish international law, few societies recognize outsiders as fully deserving of the rights and privileges they grant to their own group.

LESSON XVI

Gauls and Germans Compared

Dē Bellō Gallicō 6.24

Now It's Your Turn (pp. 138–139)

Please identify the use of the ablative in each of the following sentences.

1. *Est bōs cervī figūrā, cūius ā mediā fronte inter aurēs ūnum cornū exstitit.*
   "There is a cow in the shape of a deer, from the middle of whose forehead a single horn stands out between its ears."

   Ablative of respect

2. *Gravissimum supplicium huīc reī cum cruciātū constitūtum est.*
   "The most severe punishment with torture has been decreed for this crime."

   Ablative of accompaniment

3. *Gallī spatia omnis temporis nōn numerō diērum sed noctium fīniunt.*
   "The Gauls measure the length of all time not by the number of days but by the number of nights."

   Ablative of means

4. *Legiōnēs eōdem diē cum Quintō Titūriō āmīsit.*
   "He sent the legions with Quintus Titurius on the same day."

   Ablative of accompaninment

5. *Hāc parte Galliae pācātā tōtus et mente et animō in bellum Trēverōrum et Ambiorigis insistit.*
   "After this part of Gaul had been pacified, he concentrated entirely with both mind and spirit on the war against the Treveri and Ambiorix."

   Ablative of means

Stopping for Some Practice (p. 142)

Please identify the use of the ablative in each of the following sentences. These may not be ablatives reviewed above.

1. *Est bōs cervī figūrā, cūius ā mediā fronte inter aurēs ūnum cornū exstitit.*
   "There is a cow in the shape of a deer, from the middle of whose forehead a single horn stands out between its ears."

   Ablative of place where; ablative with the preposition

2. *Legiōnēs eōdem diē cum Quintō Titūriō āmīsit.*
   "He sent the legions with Quintus Titurius on the same day."

   Ablative of time when

3. *Ab Suebīs auxilia missa est.*
   "Auxiliary troops were sent by the Suebians."

   Ablative of agent

4. *Hāc parte Galliae pācātā tōtus et mente et animō in bellum Trēverōrum et Ambiorigis insistit.*
   "After this part of Gaul had been pacified, he concentrated entirely with both mind and spirit on the war against the Treveri and Ambiorix."

   Ablative absolute

WHAT CAESAR ACTUALLY WROTE (P. 143)

Translation

And there was earlier a time, when the Gauls excelled the Germans in respect to manliness, [when] of their own free will they waged [aggressive] wars, [when] on account of the great number of their men and the dearth of land they sent colonies across the Rhine. And those places, which are the most fertile of Germany, near the Hercynian forest, which I see was known by report to Eratosthenes and certain Greeks, which they call Orcynian, the Volcae Tectosages seized [those places (this sentence began with the direct object)] and settled there. And this [*which*] people at this time maintain themselves in these settlements and have the highest reputation for justice and military renown. Now because in the same scarcity, poverty, state of eduring hardship, in which the Germans [are], they remain, they make use of the same food and care for the body. The nearness of [our] provinces, however, to the Gauls and the knowledge of things from across the seas provides many things [*opportunities*] for abundance and consumption, [and they] little by little having become accustomed to being conquered, and having been conquered in many battles, not even they themselves compare themselves with those [Germans].

After Reading What Caesar Wrote

Thinking about How Caesar Writes (p. 143)

1. In the passage you just read, explain the use of the ablative *fāmā* in the second sentence and *virtūte* in the last sentence.

   fāmā: ablative of means

   virtūte: ablative of respect

2. What is the rhetorical effect of the asyndeton in the first (actually, first part of the last) sentence of this passage?

   in eādem inopiā, egestāte, patientiā: because the rhetorical effect of asyndeton is rapid, its use provides a sense that difficulties have been heaped up relentlessly.

3. Writers often appeal to outside authorities. Why do you think Caesar mentions Greek authors in this passage?

   Caesar alerts his readers to his own extensive knowledge, and also thereby corroborates the truth of what he writes by means of well-known experts.

Thinking about What You Read (p. 144)

These questions are provided as an aid to sparking discussions. Responses can and should vary. Our answers are by no means exhaustive.

1. If you were a Roman reader with only Caesar's description to go on, how well-informed would you feel about the Germans after reading his brief overview of their customs and way of life? Do you find his presentation convincing?

   Students may be swayed by Caesar's objective style. Everything he writes seems true. But there may be some skeptics among any group. One might ask students to cite the Latin text to explain what they found convincing and what they found less convincing. One should also ask them why they find it convincing or, on the other hand, suspect.

2. Do you think that the Romans would have been impressed that Caesar and his men were able to defeat the people he describes? Why or why not?

   Caesar paints a portrait of a tough people who operate by a code of conduct that values courage and fierce fighting. Many Romans living in the luxury and comfort of Rome would likely have found the prospect of facing such a people daunting. Caesar's audience was likely impressed.

3. Do you think that luxuries (food, drink, games that give us pleasure) weaken the ability of a society to regulate itself for the common defense? Please explain.

> Healthy food leads to healthier bodies. Drunkenness, on the other hand, leads to weakness, disease, and lack of discipline. Ancient soldiers relied on physical strength. Diet mattered. Certainly, any of these luxuries in excess is a problem and those who cannot control their appetites for luxury will not likely be able to adapt as readily to the discipline required for a common defense as would be optimal.

4. Can outside cultural influences really weaken a society? If not, why not? If so, how? Please explain.

> Most societies have feared ideas that derive from outside groups. Romans famously attempted to stamp out Christianity on the grounds that converts angered the pagan gods whom they failed to worship. The United States has historically worked with varying degrees of success at different times to stamp out or marginalize socialist ideas. Could Roman ideas of luxury really have contributed to weakness among people who adopted them?

5. What is "culture" from your perspective? And how important are language, education, religion, law, entertaintment, food, dress, and/or other elements in maintaining a cohesive and healthy society? Please explain.

> These are the constituent elements of culture, and help human beings understand who is in their group and who is outside it. One might discuss specific examples and explore why this is the case. Students may well disagree, however, as US culture is based on a rather different premise from most societies at most times. The United States has neither an official language (despite the dominance of English and a movement to make English the official language—the state of Arizona did so in 2006 and Carroll County, Maryland, did so in 2013) nor an official religion (despite the dominance of monotheisms). The United States is a society founded specifically on the rule of law, as opposed to kinship and religion, although such characteristics can help define subgroups within the United States. It is hard to tell where such a conversation might go, but it might be useful for students to compare how they construct their own cultural identity in comparison with how they view ancient cultures as described by Caesar.

LESSON XVII

THE SENATE DEBATES CAESAR

Dē Bellō Cīvīlī 1.1

Now It's Your Turn (pp. 148–149)

Translate the following conditions, taking care to adjust your translation for the tense and mood of the verbs in the protasis (if-clause or dependent clause) and apodosis (the main clause, independent clause, or "then-clause"). Please identify the type of condition, and discuss the logic of the tenses and moods of the verbs.

1. Sī senātus sequātur, Pompēius reī pūblicae nōn desit.

    If the Senate should follow, Pompey would not fail the Republic.

    Present subjunctive in both clauses; future less vivid.

2. Sī senātus sequetur, Pompēius reī pūblicae nōn deerit.

    If the Senate follows, Pompey will not fail the Republic.

    Future indicative in both clauses; future more vivid.

    NB: English uses the present in the protasis where Latin uses the future.

3. Sī senātōrēs Caesarem respiciant, Lentulus senātūs auctōritātī nōn obtemperet.

    If the senators should look to Caesar, Lentulus would not obey the authority of the Senate.

    Present subjunctive in both clauses; future less vivid.

4. Sī senātōrēs Caesarem respicient, Lentulus senātūs auctōritātī nōn obtemperābit.

    If the senators look to Caesar, Lentulus will not obey the authority of the Senate.

    Future indicative in both clauses; future more vivid.

    NB: English uses the present in the protasis where Latin uses the future.

5. Sī senātus cunctētur, nēquīquam Pompēī auxilium implōret.

   If the Senate should delay, in vain it would beg for aid from Pompey.

   Present subjunctive in both clauses; future less vivid.

6. Sī senātus cunctābitur, nēquīquam Pompēī auxilium implōrābit.

   If the Senate delays, in vain it will beg for aid from Pompey.

   Future indicative in both clauses; future more vivid.

   NB: English uses the present in the protasis where Latin uses the future.

Stopping for Some Practice (pp. 153–154)

Translate the following pairs of conditions, taking care to adjust your translation for the tense and mood of the verbs in the protasis (if-clause or dependent clause) and apodosis (the main clause, independent clause, or "then-clause"). You may want to refer to the classification of conditions in Lesson IX or in the Appendix. Please note that the sentences have been adjusted to follow the standard rules. We have eliminated the complicating factor of indirect statement in the apodosis.

1. Sī quī aut prīvātus aut populus eōrum dēcrētō nōn stetit, sacrificiīs interdīcunt.

   If anyone, either a private person or a public official, has not abided by their decree [and is thus in a present state of disobedience], they prohibit [him] from the sacrifices.

   (Perfect indicative in the protasis and present indicative in the apodosis; present general condition)

2. Sī rēs in suspīciōnem vēnit, dē uxōribus in servīlem modum quaestiōnem habent.

   If the matter is suspicious, they conduct an inquiry concerning the wives according to the method for slaves.

   (Present indicative in both clauses; present general condition)

3. Sī quis quid dē rē pūblicā ā fīnitimīs rūmōre aut fāmā accēperit, ad magistrātum dēferet.

   If anyone has heard anything concerning the Republic from neighboring peoples by gossip or report, he will bring it to the magistrate.

   (Future perfect indicative in the protasis and future indicative in the apodosis; future more vivid condition)

   NB: English idiom does not conform to the Latin tenses. It is possible to translate literally, but it would sound odd.

4. Sī Caesar exercitum nōn dīmittat, adversus rem pūblicam faciat.

   If Caesar should fail to disband his army, he would be fighting against the Republic.

   (Present tense subjunctive in both clauses; future less vivid)

5. Sī Caesar exercitum nōn dīmittet, adversus rem pūblicam faciat.

   If Caesar fails to disband his army, he will be fighting against the Republic.

   (Future indicative in both clauses; future more vivid)

   NB: English idiom does not conform to the Latin tenses. It is possible to translate literally, but it would sound odd.

What Caesar Actually Wrote (p. 155)

Translation

Caesar's letters having been given to the consuls, with difficulty it was obtained by request from them by means of the greatest struggle of the tribunes of the people that they [i.e., the letters] be read out in the Senate; that, however, a motion be made to the Senate on the basis of the letters, [this] could not be obtained by request. The consuls make a motion concerning the Republic. Lucius Lentulus, the consul, promises that he would not fail the Senate and the Republic, if boldly and bravely they should wish to state their opinions; but that if they should look to Caesar and they should pursue his favor, as they have done on previous occasions, he would take thought for himself nor would he obey the authority of the Senate: [he] considers that he too has been received into Caesar's favor and friendship. In support of the same opinion Scipio speaks: Pompey has in mind [*for Pompey it is in mind*] not to fail the Republic, if the Senate should follow; if [however] it [i.e., the Senate] should delay and act more moderately, in vain for his help, if later it should wish [his help], the Senate would beg.

After Reading What Caesar Wrote

Thinking about How Caesar Writes (pp. 155–156)

Caesar uses a variety of verbs to introduce indirect statement. He also assumes that readers can supply a verb of implied speech, thought, or perception from context when necessary. Look over the passage you just read, and identify all the places where a verb introducing indirect statement is not explicitly supplied by Caesar, but must be assumed by the reader or carried over from an earlier verb. If you have trouble, you can look back at the section "Making Sense of It" in this lesson, and, if you do have to look back, try it again on your own. The best way to understand a passage is to read it and re-read it until it begins to flow naturally as you read through it without looking at notes and vocabulary.

> **Line 2:** What is the construction (*impetrātum est*) and what are some ways to translate it? How does this clause introduce what follows?
>
>> *impetrātum est* introduces a jussive noun clause (*ut* plus the imperfect subjunctive in secondary sequence).
>
> **Line 3:** Why is it important to pay attention to the semicolon? How does it refocus the sentence as the sentence moves to its next thought?
>
>> NB: Sharp students will of course note that Caesar's original Latin text did not have a semicolon (referenced in questions for lines 3, 6, and 11) and that such punctuation was inserted by modern editors as an aid to modern readers.
>>
>> The semicolon between *recitārentur* and *ut* lets us know that the next clause is independent of what has gone before. On the other hand, because we have a semicolon rather than a full stop, we know that what comes after the semicolon will stand in close relationship with or in sharp contrast to the previous thought.
>
> **Line 6:** Again, the semicolon is a crucial guide. How does it help you understand contrasts in thought?
>
>> What comes before the semicolon represents one possibility. What comes after represents another. Caesar emphasizes this in Latin with the conjunction *sīn*. Modern typesetters use the semicolon.
>
> **Line 8:** Why do you think we inserted another *sē* in front of *habēre* in the "Making Sense of It Section" above? Can verbs of speaking in indirect statements also introduce indirect statements?
>
>> The reader must carry over the *sē* from *captūrum esse*. Caesar did not feel the need to hit readers over the head with the fact that he still reports Lentulus's argument. The *sē* after *habēre* serves as the subject of the infinitive *receptum* [*esse*].

Line 11: Again, how does the semicolon serve to organize the thought of the sentence?

> Again, the semicolon serves to join alternatives, which represent mutually exclusive possibilities.

Thinking about What You Read (p. 156)

The non-grammar based questions are provided as an aid to sparking discussions. Responses can and should vary. Our answers are by no means exhaustive.

1. Caesar portrays the consuls as worried about what Caesar will think of them. Why do you think Caesar emphasizes this?

   > Caesar had been one of the most powerful forces in Roman politics for a long time. Despite a decade in Gaul, he had kept close tabs on Roman politics, and had frequently intervened through his many agents and supporters. Cutting ties with Caesar, and risking his displeasure, would have represented a frightening prospect for many Roman politicians.

2. In the passage you just read, please identify and explain all the ablatives in the first sentence.

   > *Litterīs ... redditīs*: ablative in an absolute construction
   >
   > *summā ... contentiōne*: ablative of means
   >
   > *senātū*: ablative of place where with the preposition *in*
   >
   > *litterīs*: ablative of source with the preposition *ex*

3. Lentulus and Scipio promise their support, but only if the Senate acts boldly and without fear. This implies that the Senate is reluctant to act in this way. How does this reflect on Caesar? On the senators? On Pompey, Lentulus, and Scipio?

   > Many senators remained beholden to and/or scared of Caesar. Caesar remained powerful and a potential danger. Did senators really want to risk breaking with him? Pompey, Lentulus, and Scipio, on the other hand, are presented as bullies who compelled the reluctant senators to choose one side or the other.

4. Is it ever right to take up arms against one's own government? In 1776, Americans, who at the time were British subjects, took up arms against the British government. In 1861, the South took up arms against the federal government of the United States. How do these events compare to the civil war between Caesar and and the Roman Senate?

   > The United States was founded on the principle that sovereignty lies with the people, and that they have the right (if not the duty) to oppose tyranny. No government, however, is likely to define

itself as an unworthy tyranny. What was thus permissible in 1776 was not viewed as permissible in 1861. Had the South won, they would likely have written a history celebrating their second American Revolution. But they lost, and history is written by the victors. Such facts will help put Rome's Civil War in perspective: Caesar won. It is difficult, viewing the conflict through his prose, to view Pompey and the Senate's side sympathetically. For a diametrically opposed view, one may compare Lucan's epic on the Civil War (his *Bellum Civile* or *Pharsalia*). Pompey was Lucan's great hero.

5. The men who wrote the US Constitution studied the breakdown of the Roman Republic, and tried to structure a framework that would prevent such powerful military and political leaders as Caesar and Pompey from assuming overwhelming influence within the state through the office of the presidency. One defense they employed was the separation of powers. How similar (or not) is a president of the United States to a Roman consul or proconsul? What are some of the threats that a powerful executive poses for a republican form of government?

> The president of the United States, as commander in chief, enjoys supreme command over the military. In practice, however, the United States employs a professional army, led by powerful generals, who command the troops. The president remains a civilian, and the generals do not serve in elected office. This separation of civil and military authority, with military authority subject to civilian authority helps keep military authority in check. And Congress controls the budget of the military. The military is thus subject in effect to both the legislative and executive branches, making independent action more difficult, and making it more difficult for any individual to seize complete personal control of the military. On the other hand, an interesting constitutional development in the United States since the end of the World War II is the decreasing authority of Congress and the increasing authority of the president, who, for example, is no longer required to seek a declaration of war from Congress (although the Constitution stipulates this requirement). A Roman proconsul's powers, on the other hand, were not subject to as many checks—at least while he was in his province. If a proconsul such as Caesar left his province with his army, he represented a considerable danger to the government of the Roman Republic, precisely because he enjoyed the personal allegiance of his army.

LESSON XVIII

DISCUSSION, DEBATE, AND A DECREE AGAINST CAESAR IN THE SENATE

Dē Bellō Cīvīlī 1.2

Now It's Your Turn (p. 159)

Imperfect or perfect? Complete the following sentences by choosing the tense that makes most sense. Be prepared to justify your choice, as answers may vary.

1. Quod Caesar _____ (absum), Germānī legiōnēs _____ (oppugnō).

    aberat / oppgunābant

    Because Caesar was absent, the Germans were attacking the legions.

    Imperfect: being away and attacking are not simple actions that take place in an instant, so the imperfect is a more likely choice. If students choose the perfect, they may justify it by explaining why they view the action as completed and as a whole.

2. Marcellus ā sententiā _____ (discēdō), quod Pompēī exercitūs _____ (timēre).

    discessit / timēbat

    Marcellus departed from his proposal (i.e., changed his mind), because he was afraid of Pompey's army.

    Perfect/Imperfect: Marcellus's retreat was likely sudden and complete, his fear ongoing, hence the distinction between perfect and imperfect.

3. Quid _____ (censeō) Calidius dē eā rē?

   cēnsēbat

   What did Calidius think about this matter?

   Imperfect: Calidius's thought was likely ongoing, not complete, and thus represented as such, especially in the midst of a debate. Other choices may be justified by appropriate reference to how the student views the action. If perfect, then the action should be viewed as complete.

4. Lentulus sententiam Calidiī nōn _____ (prōnuntiō).

   prōnuntiāvit

   Lentulus did not proclaim Calidius's proposal.

   Perfect: Lentulus did not engage in the action. His inaction was thus completed in the past. It was not ongoing, although a student might make a case for the imperfect with intelligent reference to ongoing lack of action on Lentulus's part. But Lentulus will not have concerned himself with Calidius for long. He would have simply failed to put forward Calidius's motion, and moved on.

5. Senātus līberē dē eā rē dēcernere nōn _____ (audeō).

   audēbat

   The Senate did not dare to decree freely concerning this matter.

   Imperfect: the Senate's failure to be bold did not occur simply at one point during the deliberations. Their lack of nerve serves as the narrative background for the individual actions that took place during that meeting. The imperfect is used to paint just such a backdrop as this one.

Stopping for Some Practice (p. 164)

Explain the tense of each underlined verb. What is the relation of that tense to the narrator? The other action within the passage?

NB: These passages derive from your readings. Some sentences have been abbreviated for the sake of illustration.

1. Gallia <u>est</u> omnis dīvīsa in partēs trēs, quārum ūnam <u>incolunt</u> Belgae, aliam Aquītānī, tertiam quī ipsōrum linguā Celtae, nostrā Gallī <u>appellantur</u>. Hī omnēs linguā, īnstitūtīs, lēgibus inter sē <u>differunt</u>. Gallōs ab Aquītānīs Garumna flūmen, ā Belgīs Matrona et Sēquana <u>dīvidit</u>.

   Gaul is a single territory divided into three regions, one of which the Belgians inhabit, another the Aquitanians, and the third those who are called Celts in their own language and Gauls in ours. All these people differ among themselves in respect to language, customs, (and) laws. The Garonne River separates the Gauls from the Aquitanians, the Marne and the Seine divide the Gauls from the Belgians.

est: present tense because Caesar describes Gaul as it existed at the time he wrote.

incolunt: present tense because Caesar describes Gaul as it existed at the time he wrote.

appellantur: present tense because Caesar describes Gaul as it existed at the time he wrote.

differunt: present tense because Caesar describes Gaul as it existed at the time he wrote.

dīvidit: present tense because Caesar describes Gaul as it existed at the time he wrote.

2. Caesar ab decimae legiōnis cohortātiōne ad dextrum cornū profectus est, ubi suōs urgērī vīdit. Quārtae cohortis omnēs centuriōnēs occīsī erant; reliquārum cohortium, omnibus ferē centuriōnibus aut vulnerātīs aut occīsīs, in hīs prīmipīlus Publius Sextius Baculus, multīs vulneribus cōnfectus, ut iam sē sustinēre nōn posset. Reliquī erant tardiōrēs et nōn nullī proeliō excedēbant ac tēla vītābant.

After encouraging the tenth legion, Caesar set out for the right wing, where he saw that his men were being pressed. All the centurions of the fourth cohort had been killed; and almost all the centurions of the remaining cohorts were either wounded or killed, among them the centurion of the first rank Publius Sextius Baculus, having been exhausted by many wounds, with the result that he could hardly keep himself going. The remaining men were too sluggish and many were departing from the battle and avoiding the spears.

profectus est: perfect tense; simple and completed action.

vīdit: perfect tense; simple and completed action.

occīsī erant: pluperfect tense; simple action that had been completed before Caesar's arrival.

posset: imperfect subjunctive in a result clause in secondary sequence. Baculus's inability was an ongoing problem at the moment described in the narrative.

erant: imperfect; an ongoing problem during the battle in past time.

excedēbant: imperfect; ongoing and incomplete action in the past. The imperfect paints the scene.

vītābant: imperfect; ongoing and incomplete action in the past. The imperfect paints the scene.

3. Senātōrēs convīciō Lentulī correptī exagitābantur. Lentulus sē sententiam Calidiī prōnuntiātūrum esse omnīnō negāvit. Marcellus perterritus convīciīs ā suā sententiā discessit. Sīc vōcibus cōnsulis senātōrēs compulsī invītī et coactī Scīpiōnis sententiam sequuntur.

> The senators, having been scolded by Lentulus's screaming, were upset. Lentulus declared that there was no way he would announce Calidius's opinion [*put forward his motion*]. Marcellus, completely scared by the insulting screams, departed from his opinion [i.e., changed his mind]. Thus the senators, unwillingly coerced and compelled by the shouts of the consul, follow [*conform to*] Scipio's opinion.

> *exagitābantur*: imperfect; describes the ongoing condition of the senators after Lentulus yelled at them. Their distress was neither simple nor completed.

> *prōnuntiātūrum esse*: future infinitive in secondary sequence in indirect statement. This "future" represents a time that is future in relation to the past event described, but a "future" that remains past to the reader, hence "would."

> *negāvit*: Lentulus made a statement in the past. The action is viewed as simple and complete, hence perfect tense.

> *discessit*: Likewise Marcellus changed his mind: simple, complete, perfect.

> *sequuntur*: Caesar switches to the historical present. This renders the action more vivid, but also allows him to avoid using either the perfect or imperfect. The perfect would be inappropriate because the action was incomplete and ongoing. The imperfect, however, tends to put action into the narrative background. The historical present permits Caesar to focus readers' attention on key action while depicting it as an ongoing process.

What Caesar Actually Wrote (pp. 167–168)

Translation

This speech of Scipio's, because the Senate was held in the City and Pompey was absent, seemed to be sent from the very mouth of Pompey. Someone had spoken a milder opinion, as at first Marcus Marcellus, having entered into that speech, that it was not appropriate that it be formally proposed to the Senate concerning this matter before the levies had been held in all Italy and the armies had been drafted, so that with this protection [literally, "with which safe protection"] the Senate would dare to decree safely and freely what [things] it wished; as Marcus Calidius, who thought that Pompey should depart for his provinces, lest there be any ground for armed conflict: that

Caesar—two legions having been taken away from him—feared that Pompey appeared to hold and keep those [legions] near the City as a threat to him; as Marcus Rufus, who—just a few things having been changed—conformed to the opinion of Calidius. All these men, having been attacked by the loud verbal abuse of the consul Lucius Lentulus, were being insulted. Lentulus declared that there was no way he would put forward the opinion [*motion*] of Calidius. Marcellus, having been terrified by the screams, abandoned his opinion [*proposal*]. In this way, by the shouts of the consul, by fear [*sheer terror*] of the army at hand, by the threats of the friends of Pompey, very many having been compelled unwillingly and coerced, conform to the opinion of Scipio [i.e., vote for Scipio's motion]: that before a set date Caesar should dismiss his army; if he should not do this, that he would appear to be going to act against the Republic. Marcus Antonius, Quintus Cassius, the tribunes of the plebeians, [each] vetoes [the decree]. There is a motion [and debate] immediately concerning the veto of the tribunes. Harsh opinions are pronounced: as each most bitterly and cruelly has spoken, thus as much as possible he is praised by the enemies of Caesar [i.e., each is greatly praised by the enemies of Caesar to the extent that he has spoken bitterly and viciously about Caesar].

After Reading What Caesar Wrote

Thinking about How Caesar Writes (p. 168)

1. The passage you just read contains a number of verbs in the subjunctive. What tense are those verbs in? How does that tense relate to the tense of the main verb?

    conscriptī essent (line 5): pluperfect subjunctive (secondary sequence) in a subordinate clause in indirect statement.

    vellet (line 6): imperfect subjunctive (secondary sequence) in a relative clause within a relative clause of purpose that is itself subordinate in indirect statement.

    audēret (line 6): imperfect subjunctive (secondary sequence) in a relative clause of purpose.

    proficiscerētur (line 7): imperfect subjunctive (secondary sequence) in a jussive noun clause.

    esset (line 8): imperfect subjunctive (secondary sequence) in clause of negative purpose.

    dīmittat (line 17): present subjunctive (primary sequence after a main verb in the historical present) in a jussive noun clause.

    faciat (line 17): present subjunctive (primary sequence after a main verb in the historical present) in the protasis of a future less vivid condition in indirect statement.

2. Find the infinitives in indirect statement in the passage you just read. Identify the tenses of the infinitives in indirect statement, and explain their relation to the tense of the main verb.

   oportēre (line 4): present tense secondary sequence dependent on the speech implied by *ōrātiōnem* (line 4).

   timēre (line 8): present tense secondary sequence dependent on *cēnsēbat* (line 7).

3. What techniques does Caesar use to make his opponents appear irrational and unreasonable?

   Caesar represents the senators on his side as reasonable men who make moderate proposals in a spirit of compromise. Caesar represents his enemies as screamers and irrational bullies bent on his destruction.

4. A common rhetorical device in ancient literature is a figure of speech called asyndeton (Greek for "not joined"), which refers to words in a phrase not joined by a conjunction (e.g., *et* or *vel*). This device is especially effective with groups of three, which is referred to as a tricolon (Greek for "three phrases"). Abraham Lincoln used these figures in his Gettysburg address: "We cannot dedicate, we cannot consecrate, we cannot hallow, this ground." Can you find an example of both in the passage for this lesson?

   Three reasonable senators: *ut prīmō M. Marcellus . . . ; ut M. Calidius . . . ; ut M. Rūfus.*

   Three factors that determined the vote: *vōcibus . . . , terrōre . . . , minīs . . .*

5. How does Caesar's careful manipulation of imperfect, perfect, and present tenses draw readers into his narrative?

   Caesar begins the passage with imperfects that set the scene and paint the narrative backdrop. Individual acts within the context of that meeting punctuate discrete moments in the perfect tense. Caesar concludes with the historical present during the vote, the dramatic high point of the passage.

Thinking about What You Read (p. 168)

Answers will vary, and scholars still dispute these topics, so students should be encouraged to make arguments on both sides. We do provide talking points that are by no means exhaustive.

1. Caesar makes a strong case, but the law was on the side of the Senate. How unreasonable was it for the Senate to ask Caesar to dismiss his army after the successful conclusion of the war in Gaul?

    The rule of law had broken down in Rome. Caesar, Pompey, and Crassus had been ruling in effect by decree behind the scenes. For the Senate, emboldened by Pompey's military support, to insist suddenly on the rule of law, even if this were proper, was unlikely to meet with acceptance by a man as powerful as Caesar. The move was not politic. Caesar and his army too felt that their victories in Gaul merited respect and customary rewards.

2. Even people as powerful as senators sometimes feel pressured into supporting programs they do not truly believe in. What would you consider the most common pressures facing politicians today? Do you think these same pressures mattered in ancient Rome?

    Today, critics note that the increasingly high cost of running a campaign for office makes politicians more beholden to their donors than ever before. Politicians are also under pressure to make sure that they help channel government investment to their districts—thus, they support "pork barrel" projects or fight the closure of military bases irrespective of their usefulness. The senators in Rome faced Pompey's soldiers who were camped just outside Rome. Caesar's soldiers were far away. And the consuls, supported by Pompey, were yelling at them in public. Bullies can be powerful, especially when backed by an army!

3. Why is it harder to state your true feelings and opinions in front of a large group as opposed to a small circle of friends? Do you think that ancient Roman politicians dealt with similar challenges in expressing their opinions? Please explain.

    Students will likely have experienced social and peer pressures. They should be encouraged to make comparisons.

LESSON XIX

ABUSED TRIBUNES AND INSULTS TO CAESAR'S PERSONAL DIGNITY

Dē Bellō Cīvīlī 1.7

Now It's Your Turn (pp. 170–171)

Please identify the genitive construction:

1. Omnēs, quī sunt ēius ordinis, ēvocantur.

   ēius ordinis: genitive of quality

   All who are [members] of this rank are summoned.

2. Multī spē praemiōrum ēvocantur.

   praemiōrum: objective genitive

   Many are attracted by the hope of rewards.

3. Amīcī consulum in senātum cōguntur.

   consulum: possessive genitive

   The friends of the consuls are forced into [i.e., compelled to come to] the Senate.

4. Veterēs inimīcitiae Caesaris Catōnem incitant.

   Caesaris: objective genitive

   Ancient hatred of Caesar motivates Cato.

5. Gallia est omnis dīvīsa in partēs trēs, quārum ūnam incolunt Belgae.

   quārum: partitive genitive

   Gaul is a whole divided into three parts, of which [parts] the Belgians inhabit one.

Stopping for Some Practice (pp. 175–176)

Please translate each sentence, and identify the genitive constructions.

1. Eōrum fīnēs Nerviī attingēbant.

    The Nervii extended to their boundaries [i.e., Nervian territory extended to their borders].

    Eōrum: possessive genitive

2. Eārum rērum magnam partem temporis brevitās et incursus hostium impediēbat.

    The shortness of time and the invasion of enemies interfered with a large portion of these things.

    Eārum rērum: partitive genitive

    temporis: descriptive genitive

    hostium: subjective genitive

3. Caesar ab decimae legiōnis cohortātiōne ad dextrum cornū profectus est.

    Caesar went from encouraging the tenth legion to the right wing.

    decimae legiōnis: objective genitive

4. Druidēs mīlitiae vacātiōnem omniumque rērum habent immūnitātem.

    The Druids have an exemption from military service and immunity in all matters.

    mīlitiae: objective genitive

    omniumque rērum: objective genitive

5. Ab consulibus impetrātum est summā tribūnōrum plebis contentiōne, ut in senātū litterae Caesaris recitārentur.

    It was obtained by request from the consuls by means of the greatest struggle of the tribunes of the plebeians that the letters of Caesar be read out in the Senate.

    tribūnōrum plebis: subjective genitive

    Caesaris: possessive genitive

What Caesar Actually Wrote (p. 177)

Translation

And with these things having been ascertained, Caesar speaks in assembly among his soldiers. He recalls the wrongs of all times that his enemies did to him, by whom he complains that Pompey has been led astray and corrupted by jealousy and slander of his [Caesar's] fame, whose [i.e., Pompey's] honor and status he himself [Caesar] has always promoted and been a supporter of. He complains that a revolutionary precedent has been set in the Republic, that the tribunician veto was annulled and suppressed by armed force, which [i.e., the tribunician veto] had been restored in previous years by armed force. Sulla—tribunician power having been stripped in respect of all matters—nevertheless had left the veto free. Pompey, who seems to have restored lost things [or "grants"; i.e., the former powers of the tribunes], had taken away even the grants [i.e., the vestiges of power], which they had before . . . He [Caesar] urges that they [the soldiers] defend from his enemies the reputation and status of the commander, by means of whose leadership [*of him, by means of which commander's leadership*] for nine years they most fortunately managed the Republic and accomplished very many successful wars, [and under whose leadership] all Gaul and Germany they have pacified. The soldiers of the thirteenth legion, which was present, shout—for this [legion] he had called out at the beginning of the uprising, and the others had not yet arrived—that they are ready to repel the wrongs against their commander and the tribunes of the plebeians.

After Reading What Caesar Wrote

Thinking about How Caesar Writes (p. 178)

Line 1: What is the tense of *contiōnātur*? Why?

> Historical present: Caesar narrates a key moment, his decision to make war against the Senate.

Line 2: Why is *ā quibus* in the ablative?

> Ablative of agent

Lines 5–7: Can you name and explain the four ablative constructions in this sentence?

> *rē pūblicā*: ablative of place where.
>
> *armīs*: ablative of means.
>
> *superiōribus annīs*: ablative of time when.
>
> *armīs*: ablative of means.

Lines 10–13: Can you explain the use of the genitive in these lines?

cūius imperātōris: **subjective genitive.**

ēius: **possessive genitive.**

Lines 13–16: What kinds of genitives do you find in these lines?

legiōnis: **possessive genitive.**

tumultūs: **objective genitive.**

imperātōris suī tribūnōrumque plēbis: **objective genitive.**

1. As you may recall, a common feature of Latin style is ellipsis (sometimes called "gapping") or leaving out a word that has already been mentioned (this is common in English too) or one that you will encounter later in the sentence (this is much less common in English). Can you find examples of ellipsis in the passage you just read?

    Pompēium, quī āmissa [dōna] restituisse videātur, dōna etiam, quae ante habuerint, adēmisse **(lines 9–10).**

    Conclāmant legiōnis XIII, quae aderat, mīlitēs—hanc [legiōnem] enim initiō tumultūs ēvocāverat, reliquae [legiōnēs] nōndum convēnerant **(lines 13–15).**

2. How does Caesar's speech to his soldiers compare to the meeting of the Senate Caesar described? How does he make himself appear more reasonable than his opponents?

    Caesar presents facts, for example, the wrongs done to him, or the victories won by himself and his soldiers. He does not scream or abuse.

3. When making a case on one's own behalf, speakers sometimes exaggerate points in their own favor. How objective do you think Caesar was in representing his own position?

    Answers will vary. Students should cite the Latin to explain their answers.

4. What are some Latin words in the passage you just read that refer to a sense of personal worth or one's reputation? How important do you think public appearance was to Rome's leaders?

    laudis **(line 4)**

    honōrī **(line 4)**

    dignitātī **(line 4)**

    existimātiōnem **(line 13)**

    dignitātem **(line 13)**

Appearance, status, and personal dignity played crucially important roles in Roman politics. Avoidance of shame was in general a primary motivation in the ancient world.

5. In the passage you just read, please identify a jussive noun clause and a result clause, and explain the tense of the subjunctive.

    Purpose: *intrōductum exemplum [esse] queritur, ut . . . notārētur atque opprimerētur.* (lines 5–6)

    Imperfect subjunctives in secondary sequence after the historical present of the main verb *queritur* because the infinitive of the indirect statement (which is past) puts the sequence definitively in the past and hence secondary sequence.

    Jussive noun clause: *Hortātur . . . ut . . . dēfendant.* (lines 10–13)

    Present subjunctive in primary sequence after the historical present *hortātur*. This choice maintains the sequence in relation to that main verb, and thus keeps readers involved in the "present drama."

6. The passage you just read contains some verbs in the pluperfect indicative. Please explain how those verbs relate to what else happened in the past.

    These verbs relate action in the past that preceded other actions in the past.

Thinking about What You Read (p. 178)

These questions are provided as an aid to sparking discussions. Responses can and should vary. Our answers are by no means exhaustive.

1. Politics in a democratic or republican form of government often involve compromise that satisfies neither side. Are there times when it is justified to adopt a position that will accept no compromise whatsoever or "zero tolerance" for the other side?

    If compromise involves violating people's rights, then compromise is probably undesirable. The political compromise, for example, that counted slaves as three-fifths of a person induced southern states to sign onto a constitution that would otherwise have given more political power to states with larger populations of free citizens. Most people today, however, view that compromise as immoral, and one that eventually contributed to one of the most murderous wars in human history, the US Civil War. Other compromises, for example, on taxes and spending or on farm subsidies, usually do not arouse similar passions (except, of course, when they do). A refusal to compromise, however, can lead to dangerous instability, so compromise remains one of the great arts of politics.

2. What are the advantages of political compromise?

   All sides get something that they want.

3. What are the disadvantages of political compromise?

   One side getting anything at all may be unacceptable to the other side. A partial victory is an incomplete victory.

LESSON XX

Pompey and Labienus Abuse their Victory over Caesar

Dē Bellō Cīvīlī 3.71

Now It's Your Turn (pp. 180–181)

Identify the participle in each sentence, translate the sentence literally, and then translate the sentence again, but turning the participle into a subordinate clause.

1. Labiēnus omnēs captīvōs prōductōs ostentātiōnis causā interfēcit.

   prōductōs: perfect passive participle

   Literally: For the sake of a demonstration, Labienus killed all the prisoners having been led out.

   Better: For the sake of a demonstration, Labienus killed all the prisoners who had been led out.

2. Labiēnus omnēs captīvōs commīlitōnēs appellāns interfēcit.

   appellāns: present active participle

   Literally: Labienus, calling [them] "fellow soldiers," killed all the prisoners.

   Better: Although he called them "fellow soldiers," Labienus killed all the prisoners.

3. Labiēnus omnēs captīvōs magnā verbōrum contumēliā interrogāns, solērentne mīlitēs fugere, interfēcit.

   interrogāns: present active participle

   Literally: Labienus, asking all the prisoners with a great harrangue of words, whether solders were accustomed to running away, killed [them].

   Better: Labienus, who with a great harrangue of words asked all the prisoners whether soldiers were in the habit of running away, killed them.

For the following sentences, please identify as many verbal behaviors as you can for each of the present participles.

4. Labiēnus omnēs captīvōs commīlitōnēs appellāns interfēcit.

   Tense: because a present participle takes place at the same time as the main verb, we know that the "hailing" (*appellāns*) took place in the past, as *interfēcit* is in the perfect tense.

   Subject: *Labiēnus* (masculine nominative singular) serves as the subject of *appellāns* (masculine nominative singular).

   Direct Object: we may read *omnēs captīvōs* (accusative plural) as the direct object of *appellāns* and *commīlitōnēs* as the attributive noun in apposition with the direct object, i.e., one calls "x" "y."

5. Labiēnus omnēs captīvōs magnā verbōrum contumēliā interrogāns, solērentne mīlitēs fugere, interfēcit.

   Tense: because a present participle takes place at the same time as the main verb, we know that the "asking" (*interrogāns*) took place in the past, as *interfēcit* is in the perfect tense.

   Subject: *Labiēnus* (masculine nominative singular) serves as the subject of *interrogāns* (masculine nominative singular).

   Direct Object: we may read *omnēs captīvōs* (accusative plural) as the direct object of *interrogāns*.

   Adverbial Phrase: the ablative of means (with its objective genitive) *magnā verbōrum contumēliā* tells us how Labienus was asking his question.

   Indirect Question: the indirect question *solērentne mīlitēs fugere* introduced by *interrogāns* uses secondary sequence because present participles happen at the same time as the main verb, in this case *interfēcit*, which is in the past tense.

Stopping for Some Practice (pp. 185–186)

Identify the participle in each sentence, translate the sentence literally, and then translate the sentence again, but turning the participle into a subordinate clause. (We have adapted sentences from the previous two sections for some additional vocabulary review.)

1. Hīs rēbus cognitīs, Caesar apud mīlitēs contiōnātur.

   Participle: *cognitīs* (perfect passive)

   Literally: These matters having been ascertained, Caesar holds an assembly among his soldiers.

   Better: After Caesar *was* informed of these things, he *addresses* his soldiers in an assembly.

2. Hīs rēbus cognitīs, Caesar apud mīlitēs contiōnātus est.

   Participle: *cognitīs* (perfect passive)

   Literally: These matters having been ascertained, Caesar held an assembly among his soldiers.

   Better: After Caesar *had been* informed of these things, he *addressed* his soldiers in an assembly.

3. Marcellus perterritus convīciīs ā suā sententiā discēdit.

   Participle: *perterritus* (perfect passive)

   Literally: Marcellus, terrified by the abuse, departed from his opinion.

   Better: Marcellus, who *was* terrified by the abuse, *changes* his vote.

4. Marcellus perterritus convīciīs ā suā sententiā discessit.

   Participle: *perterritus* (perfect passive)

   Literally: Marcellus, terrified by the abuse, departed from his opinion.

   Better: Marcellus, who *had been* terrified by the abuse, *changed* his vote.

5. Omnēs, vōcibus consulis compulsī, Scipiōnis sententiam sequuntur.

   Participle: *compulsī* (perfect passive)

   Literally: All [the senators], coerced by the shouts of the consul, conform to Scipio's opinion.

   Better: Because they *were* coerced by the shouts of the consul, all [the senators] *conform* to Scipio's opinion.

6. Omnēs, vōcibus consulis compulsī, Scipiōnis sententiam secūtī sunt.

   Participle: *compulsī* (perfect passive)

   Literally: All [the senators], coerced by the shouts of the consul, conformed to Scipio's opinion.

   Better: Because they *had been* coerced by the shouts of the consul, all [the senators] *conformed* to Scipio's opinion.

What Caesar Actually Wrote (p. 187)

Translation

In the two battles of this single day, Caesar lost nine hundred soldiers and well-known Romans [i.e., Roman citizens] of the Equestrian class: Tuticanus the "Gaul," the son of a senator, Gaius Fleginas from Placentia, Aulus Granius from Puteoli, Marcus Sacrativir from Capua, thirty-two tribunes of the soldiers and centurions; but of all these men the large part [i.e., the majority], having been overwhelmed in the ditches and fortifications and on the banks of the river, in terror of their own men and in flight perished without any wound; and thirty-two military standards were lost. Pompey was hailed as *imperator* [*victorious commander*] in that battle. He kept this title and allowed himself to be hailed in this manner afterward, but neither was he accustomed to write [the title] in his letters nor did he place the tokens of the laurel branch in his *fasces* [the insignia of his command]. But Labienus, when he had obtained from him [Pompey] by request, that he [Pompey] command that the prisoners be handed over to himself [Labienus], all [the prisoners], having been lead out, as it seemed, for the sake of a demonstration, so that greater credibility would be held for [i.e., granted to] a traitor [i.e., by Pompey to Labienus], calling [them] fellow soldiers, and asking [them] with a great harrangue of words, whether veteran soldiers were accustomed to run away, he killed [them] in plain sight of all.

After Reading What Caesar Wrote

Thinking about How Caesar Writes (p. 188)

1. Caesar's style, which at first glance appears plain and matter-of-fact, actually conveys rather powerfully (and potentially even emotionally for his readers) Caesar's point of view. Caesar's rhetoric suggests that he, Caesar, fights for Italy, whereas his opponents, Pompey and Labienus, aim instead to slaughter Roman citizens, the one for personal glory, the other for even baser reasons. How does Caesar accomplish this rhetorical feat? Please examine carefully how he portrays himself (and not saying much about oneself represents a portrait too) and his own men versus how he portrays the conduct of Pompey and Labienus.

   Points to consider: Caesar emphasizes that his soldiers are Roman citizens from all parts of Italy. Caesar has lost rank and file as well as distinguished men and veteran commanders. He concedes that he has suffered a grievous defeat. Pompey, however, allows himself to be decorated for the slaughter of Roman citizens. Labienus, Caesar's great lieutenant from the Gallic wars, is now called a "traitor," who exults in the slaughter of Roman citizens in a sycophantic effort to gain credibility with his new master, Pompey. Caesar begins with sorrow, moves to incredulity, and concludes with outrage.

2. How do specific examples of Roman *equitēs* who served with Caesar help personalize Caesar's losses?

   Points to consider: Caesar provides individual names. He tells his readers where the men are from. Their diversity would serve to emphasize that all Romans, no matter whose side they were on, would suffer personal loss.

3. How do numbers help us grasp the scope of Caesar's defeat? How many days? Battles? Men lost? Standards lost? etc.

   Points to consider: Because they are basic and concrete, numbers help readers imagine the scope of the loss. Quantity and length may be pictured with greater precision. "Thirty-two standards" are different from "many standards." Someone took the time to count. So, also, with the loss of lives. Caesar portrays his accuracy and his concern for details and for individuals. Even numbers can be rhetorical.

4. Compare the portrayals of Pompey and Labienus in this passage. How similar to or different from each other are they? Why?

   Points to consider: Caesar always accords Pompey a measure of respect. Until he is dead, most Romans would have thought of Pompey, not Caesar, as the greatest man in Rome. Pompey was also the leader of a majority of the senators, the leading men in Rome. Caesar would need to win them back after the war, if he survived, which was by no means guaranteed. Pompey was, in short, to be respected. Caesar does not refrain from pointing out what represents in his view errors on Pompey's part (accepting the title *imperator* for the defeat of fellow citizens), but he does so with a sense of regret, and he generally attributes much of the blame to those around Pompey rather than to the great man himself, thus leaving Pompey, should he so choose, room to maneuver and find a way to cut a deal with Caesar (which, in Roman politics, was never out of the question). Labienus, on the other hand, had abandoned Caesar, who had relied on him as his most faithful lieutenant. The hatred and bitterness of these two men for each other was irreconcilable. Caesar depicts Labienus as a bloodthirsty and cruel murderer, a psychopathic toady.

5. Please identify every participle in this passage and identify how it is used. For example, as an adjective, part of a compound verb, as a subordinate clause, etc.

   nōtōs (line 2) [perfect masculine accusative plural participle]: "well-known," used as an adjective to describe the *equitēs* [masuline accusative plural].

   oppressa (line 6) [perfect feminine nominative singular participle in agreement with *pars*]: despite the literal translation given above for the sake of syntactical clarity, this participle would be best treated as a subordinate thought and thus translated as a subordinate clause.

   amissa (line 8) [perfect neuter nominative plural participle in agreement with the subject *signa*]: perfect passive compound verb with *sunt*.

   appellātus (line 9) [perfect masculine nominative singular participle in agreement with the subject *Pompēius*]: perfect passive compound verb with *est*.

   passus (line 9) [perfect masculine nominative singular participle in agreement with the unexpressed subject *Pompēius*]: perfect passive compound verb with *est*.

solitus (line 10) [perfect masculine nominative singular participle in agreement with the unexpressed subject *Pompēius*]: perfect passive compound verb with *est*.

prōductōs (line 12) [perfect passive masculine accusative plural participle in agreement with *omnēs*]: despite the literal translation given above for the sake of syntactical clarity, this participle would be best treated as a subordinate thought and thus translated as a subordinate clause.

appellāns (line 13) [present active masculine nominative singular participle in agreement with the unexpressed subject *Labiēnus*]: despite the literal translation given above for the sake of syntactical clarity, this participle would be best treated as a subordinate thought and thus translated as a subordinate clause.

interrogāns (line 14) [present active masculine nominative singular participle in agreement with the unexpressed subject *Labiēnus*]: despite the literal translation given above for the sake of syntactical clarity, this participle would be best treated as a subordinate thought and thus translated as a subordinate clause.

Thinking about What You Read (p. 188)

These questions are provided as an aid to sparking discussions. Responses can and should vary. Our answers are by no means exhaustive.

1. Please explain in what ways a civil war is different from a war against foreign enemies.

    In a civil war, people who consider themselves related, a "family" of sorts, kill people they recognize as fully human. It is more difficult to kill those with whom we identify than it is to kill foreigners whom we often fear (or even actively dislike) because we do not understand their language, culture, values, or religion.

2. Civil wars erupt when societies can no longer settle differences through a well-regulated political process. What were the political and personal divisions between Caesar's faction and the Senate? (This may require a bit of research.) Can you think of differences that have led to civil war in other places and times? How were (or are) these civil wars similar to and different from the Rome's civil war?

    More details will make the discussion more interesting, but Caesar's enemies in the Senate did not want to grant Caesar a post-Gaul role in government. They were out to ruin him completely because they thought that, with Pompey's support, they could. Caesar's faction wanted what Caesar could, if he continued to enjoy a role in Roman government, deliver to them in terms of

legislation, offices, and debt relief. Had the senatorial faction won, and rid themselves of Caesar, would the Senate have been able to dispense with Pompey in turn? We cannot know. The most obvious comparison to Rome's civil war is the US Civil War. Lincoln offered various compromises. Why did the South refuse?

LESSON XXI

Pride before the Fall? The Pompeians Celebrate their Victory

Dē Bellō Cīvīlī 3.72

Now It's Your Turn (pp. 190–191)

Translate each sentence, identify the preposition, and explain why it governs the case that it does.

1. Marcus Marcellus in eam ōrātiōnem ingressus est.

    Marcus Marcellus entered into [began] this speech.

    in: accusative. Although Marcus Marcellus did not actually move in physical space from point A to point B, the verb "entered" implies such motion, hence accusative.

2. Caesar iniūriās inimīcōrum in sē commemorat.

    Caesar recalls the wrongs [done] by enemies against himeslf.

    in: accusative. This is a tough one, as *sē* could be ablative or accusative. But what makes more sense metaphorically: ablative of place where or accusative of motion toward? A survey of republican Latin usage actually reveals some evidence for the ablative, but the accusative predominates.

3. Pompēius in fascibus insignia laureae nōn praetulit.

    Pompey did not put on display the decorations of laurel in his *fascēs* [the insignia of his command].

    in: ablative of place where

4. Labiēnus mīlitēs in omnium conspectū interfēcit.

    Labienus killed the soldiers in the plain view of all.

    in: ablative of place where

5. Pars magna exercitūs in fossās coacta est.

   A large part of the army was forced into the ditches.

   in: accusative of motion toward which

6. Pars magna exercitūs in fossīs oppressa est.

   A large part of the army was overwhelmed in the ditches.

   in: ablative of place where or within which

7. Pars magna exercitūs sine ullō vulnere interiit.

   A large part of the army perished without any wound.

   sine: this preposition takes the ablative exclusively.

Stopping for Some Practice (pp. 195–196)

Put the word in parentheses into the proper case, translate the sentence, and explain your choice.

1. Ab [consulēs] impetrātum est, ut Caesaris litterae in [senātus] recitārentur.

   From the consuls it was obtained by request that Caesar's letter be read aloud in the Senate.

   Ab consulibus: ablative with *ab* (the consuls represent the source of the authority for the reading).

   Without context, one might also translate this as an ablative of agent, that is, "it was gained by request by the consuls that," etc. But what authority was there in the Senate higher than the consuls? Whom would they have asked? This translation, while grammatically possible, is absurd in the Republican period. A clever student might rejoin, however, that under the empire consuls might have to ask "Caesar," that is, the emperor, for permission to read "Caesar's" letter aloud in the Senate. That student would have a good point, but the teacher may point out that this Reader has hitherto offered no imperial examples, so that interpretation, while somewhat more plausible, still falls short.

   in senātū: ablative of place where or within which

2. Ut ex [litterae] ad [senātus] referrētur, impetrārī nōn potuit.

   That according to the letter a motion be made to the Senate, it could not be obtained by request.

   ex litterīs: ablative with *ex*

   ad senātum: accusative with *ad*

3. Referunt consulēs dē [rēs pūblica].

   The consuls make a motion concerning the Republic.

   dē rē pūblicā: ablative with *dē*.

4. In [eadem sententia] loquitur Scīpiō.

   Scipio speaks to the same opinion [i.e., in favor of the proposal].

   in eandem sententiam: accusative of motion toward, although the motion is merely metaphorical. One speaks from one point in the direction of another.

5. Marcellus ā [sua sententia] discessit.

   Marcellus departed from his opinion. [I.e., Marcellus changed his mind, his vote, etc.]

   ā suā sententiā: ablative of place from which or ablative with *ab*.

What Caesar Actually Wrote (p. 197)

Translation

By means of these things [i.e., recent victories] so much confidence [partitive genitive] and enthusiasm accrued to the Pompeians that they did not think about the logic of war, but they seemed already to have won. They considered that the cause was [*that there was for a cause*] not the fewness of our soldiers, not the unevenness of the ground and the narrow [spaces]—the camps having been seized beforehand—and the twofold terror both inside and outside the fortification, not the army having been split into two parts, when one [part] was unable to bring help to the other part. Nor did they add to these [factors] that it had been fought not with a bitter coming together [i.e., the clash of opposing battle lines in set formation], [and that it had been fought] not by means of a [set] battle, and that they themselves [i.e., Caesar's soldiers] had brought more harm to themselves by their numerousness and because of the narrow [spaces], than they had received from the enemy. Nor finally did they recall the common misfortunes of war, how so often small occasions of either false worry or of sudden terror or of religion thrown in the way [i.e., a religious consideration or obligation that would pose an obstacle to action] had inflicted great damages, how many times it had been blundered in an army [*an army had blundered*] by the mistake of a general or through the fault of a tribune; but [instead], just as if by means of manliness they had won, [and as if] no change in affairs could [*nor could any change in affairs*] take place, throughout the whole wide world they were trumpeting [*making well known*] the victory of that day by report and letters.

LESSON XXI

AFTER READING WHAT CAESAR WROTE

Thinking about How Caesar Writes (p. 198)

1. Caesar uses rhetoric to argue that the Pompeian victory was not as significant as the Pompeians claimed. What are some of the key features of Caesar's verbal artistry in this passage? His logic?

   Points to consider: Caesar argues that the true mettle of his army had not been tested, as they were beaten not in bravery but by circumstances, which he enumerates in detail. The Pompeians, however, attribute their victory to their own bravery, and fail to appreciate all the things that can go wrong in battle. The logic is, of course, true to an extent (sometimes luck is against one's efforts), but also self-serving. Why had Caesar not planned for these contingencies? On the other hand, believing that a battle is over before it truly is can definitely be dangerous, as the Pompeians will learn to their cost.

2. Identify the verbs in this passage that appear in the subjunctive, and explain the the reasons for both tense and mood.

   cōgitārent (line 2): imperfect subjunctive secondary sequence in a clause of positive result.

   vidērentur (line 2): imperfect subjunctive secondary sequence in a clause of positive result.

   posset (line 6): imperfect subjunctive (secondary sequence) in a *cum* temporal clause.

   accēpissent (line 9): pluperfect subjunctive (secondary sequence) in a subordinate clause in indirect statement dependent on *addēbant* (line 7).

   intulissent (line 12): pluperfect subjunctive (secondary sequence) in a subordinate clause in indirect statement dependent on *recordābantur*.

   esset offēnsum (lines 12–13): pluperfect subjunctive (secondary sequence) in a subordinate clause in indirect statement dependent on *recordābantur*.

   vīcissent (line 13): pluperfect subjunctive (secondary sequence) in the protasis of what would have been a past contrary to fact condition that is, however, instead being used to make a comparison in what is a mixed condition. Compare: "If they had conquered, they would have celebrated" with "They celebrated, just as if they had won."

posset (line 14): imperfect subjunctive (secondary sequence) in the protasis of what would have been a past contrary to fact condition that is, however, instead being used to make a comparison in what is a mixed condition. Compare: "If no change of affairs could take place, they would have celebrated" with "They celebrated, just as if no change of affairs could take place."

3. What participles in this passage are used where we would use subordinate clauses in English? Translate each participle literally, and then formulate an equivalent subordinate clause.

   <u>*praeoccupātīs*</u> *castrīs* (line 4): the camp having been occuppied beforehand (ablative absolute); because the camp had been seized beforehand.

   <u>*abscīsum*</u> *in duās partēs exercitum* (line 5): the army having been split into two parts; the army that had been split into two parts.

   <u>*obiectae*</u> *religiōnis* (line 11): religion having been thrown in the way; religion, which had become an obstacle.

4. The descriptive genitive combines an adjective with a noun to explain or describe a quality of the noun, on which the descriptive phrase depends. Find examples of descriptive genitives in this passage.

   falsae suspīciōnis (line 10): descriptive genitive with *causae*

   terrōris repentīnī (line 11): descriptive genitive with *causae*

   obiectae religiōnis (line 11): descriptive genitive with *causae*

Thinking about What You Read (p. 198)

These are open-ended questions, so answers can and should vary. Students should be encouraged both to use evidence from the text and to think more broadly about the issues raised, especially through any comparisons they might be able to make to analagous historical or even contemporary situations. Our answers are by no means exhaustive.

1. Why was it important for Caesar to minimize the importance of his defeat? Please explain.

   Caesar was the underdog. Much of his success depended on what people believed was going to happen and the willingness of his supporters to continue supporting him. If their confidence was shaken, they might begin working on coming to terms with the other side.

2. How important is the perception of how well or badly a war is going for the eventual outcome of that war? Does perception play a similar role in political campaigns? A sporting event? Does public opinion matter? Why or why not?

> **Public perception is often self-fulfilling. The economy, for example, sometimes prospers because people and businesses feel confident. When they lose confidence, the economy falters. People are more likely to surrender if they feel that the other side's victory is inevitable. Shaping public opinion is part of a more general war effort.**

3. Do you think that Caesar's men needed cheering up after their defeat? How is serving as the general of an army similar to or different from coaching a team? leading a company? Please explain.

> **Defeat is disheartening and can lead to a desire to surrender. The general, like a coach, or any other leader, must work to keep the group confident that future success is still possible.**

4. What means did Caesar use to combat the "celebration" of the Pompeians? Do you think that the passage you just read would have been effective among Caesar's readers in Rome? With the men in his own army? Please explain.

> **Caesar does his best to explain his defeat, and it may well have convinced some or at least calmed some fears, but a general was only as good as his last battle. Caesar would need a new victory to completely vindicate this defeat.**

LESSON XXII

Victory or Death: Labienus Insults Caesar and Swears an Oath

Dē Bellō Cīvīlī 3.87

Now It's Your Turn (p. 201)

In the following *cum*-clauses, identify whether the verb is in the subjunctive or indicative. If the verb is subjunctive, try translating the *cum* clauses as an adversative (concessive), a causal, and a temporal clause. Decide which translation is best, and explain why you think you have chosen the best option. Do some of the examples remain ambiguous? Why? Which of the following *cum* clauses **must** you translate as a *cum* temporal clause? Why? Can you translate the indicative examples both as a simple date and as repeated action? Why or why not?

1. <u>Cum</u> Caesar causam <u>quaereret</u>, sīc reperiēbat: nullum esse aditum ad eōs mercātōribus.

    Cum . . . quaereret: imperfect subjunctive (secondary sequence).

    Cum causal: Because Caesar asked about the cause, thus he discovered: there was no access for them to merchants [i.e., they had no access to merchants and their wares].

    Cum adversative: Although Caesar asked about the cause, thus he discovered: there was no access for them to merchants.

    Cum temporal: When Caesar asked about the cause, thus he discovered: there was no access for them to merchants.

    Cum temporal makes the most sense, as one usually gets answers *when* one inquires. In fact, it is really the only good possibility. Some students may, however, make a case for *cum*-causal, which is possible, but begs the question. Was the answer foreordained? *Cum*-adversative, on the other hand, is absurd.

2. <u>Cum</u> sē in castra <u>reciperent</u>, hostibus occurrēbant.

   Cum ... reciperent: imperfect subjunctive (secondary sequence).

   Cum causal: Because they betook themselves back into the camp, they encountered the enemy.

   Cum adversative: Although they betook themselves back into the camp, they encountered the enemy.

   Cum temporal: When they betook themselves back into the camp, they encountered the enemy.

   Cum adversative is best, as one does not expect to run into the enemy when retreating into the safety of one's camp. On the other hand, *cum*-temporal is certainly possible, as the encounter took place during the flight. *Cum*-causal on the other hand would make little sense, unless the context created a situation where they were perhaps in search of the enemy in the camp.

3. <u>Cum</u> hostēs in nostrīs castrīs versārī <u>vīdissent</u>, praecipitēs fugae sēsē mandābant.

   Cum ... vīdissent: pluperfect subjunctive (secondary sequence).

   Cum causal: Because they had seen that the enemy was roaming about in our camp, they were throwing themselves headlong into flight.

   Cum adversative: Although they had seen that the enemy was roaming about in our camp, they were throwing themselves headlong into flight.

   Cum temporal: When they had seen that the enemy was roaming about in our camp, they were throwing themselves headlong into flight.

   Cum causal best explains why they ran away. *Cum*-temporal is certainly possible as the timing would be right. *Cum*-adversative, however, would be illogical.

4. <u>Cum</u> paterfamiliae nātus <u>dēcessit</u>, ēius propinquī conveniunt.

   Cum ... dēcessit: present perfect indicative (primary sequence).

   Whenever the son of the head of the household has died, his relatives assemble.

   Repeated action makes more sense. It is difficult to conceive how we could construe this as a simple time and date with the main clause in the present tense.

5. Cum bellum cīvitās infert, magistrātūs dēliguntur.

    Cum ... infert: present indicative (primary sequence).

    Whenever a state wages war, leaders are chosen.

    Repeated action makes more sense. It is difficult to conceive how we could construe this as a simple time and date with the main clause in the present tense.

6. Cum Caesaris cōpiās despiceret, Labiēnus negāvit hunc esse exercitum, quī Galliam dēvīcerit.

    Cum ... despiceret: imperfect subjunctive (secondary sequence).

    Cum causal: Because he disparaged Caesar's troops, Labienus claimed that this was not the army that conquered Gaul.

    Cum adversative: Although he disparaged Caesar's troops, Labienus claimed that this was not the army that conquered Gaul.

    Cum temporal: When he was disparaging Caesar's troops, Labienus claimed that this was not the army that conquered Gaul.

    Cum causal makes the most sense, as it explains why Labienus claimed that Caesar's army was not the same one that conquered Gaul. *Cum* temporal, however, is possible. *Cum* adversative would make no sense, as it would contradict what we read in the main clause.

Stopping for Some Practice (pp. 207–208)

Put the verb in square brackets into an appropriate tense of the subjunctive, and translate the sentence. Discuss which variety of *cum*-clause you find most convincing. Try rendering the verb as an indicative. Does the sentence still make sense? If the answer is yes, how has the meaning changed? Is the indicative superior to the subjunctive in some instances? Why or why not?

1. Cum ad arma concurrī [oportet], ab opere Caesar revocāvit mīlitēs.

    Cum ... opportēret: imperfect subjunctive (secondary sequence).

    Cum-causal: Because it was opportune for there to be a running for weapons [i.e., for battle to be engaged], Caesar called the soldiers back from the work [on the fortification]. As is so often the case, *cum* temporal would be possible too.

    Cum ... opportēbat: imperfect indicative (secondary sequence).

    As many times as it was opportune for there to be a running for weapons [i.e., for battle to be engaged], Caesar called the soldiers back from the work [on the fortification].

Cum ... opportuit: perfect indicative (secondary sequence).

At the time it was opportune for there to be a running for weapons [i.e., for battle to be engaged], Caesar called the soldiers back from the work [on the fortification]. This simple date and time with indicative helps us understand why *cum ... opportēret* (above) is more likely to be construed as causal. The timing motivated Caesar's action. The indicative, while theoretically possible, does not work at all in terms of sense.

NB: We will not repeat this exercise below, as we do not want to drill inappropriate responses. This is best discussed once or twice with an emphasis on what makes most sense, not on what may be theoretically possible.

2. Instructus est exercitus ut locī nātūra postulābat, cum legiōnēs hostibus [resistō].

    Cum ... resistērent: imperfect subjunctive (secondary sequence).

    cum causal: The army was drawn up as the nature of the place [*the lay of the land*] required, as the legions were putting up a fight against the enemy.

    One might make a case for the imperfect indicative (*resistēbant*), if this were a theoretical discussion of past strategy, but it would be rather unlikely. The imperfect would not make sense, as, again, there is too much cause and effect involved to render this thought as a simple statement about generally repeated action.

3. Cum altera alterī auxilium ferre nōn [possum], duae partēs exercitūs effugiēbant.

    Cum ... posset: imperfect subjunctive (secondary sequence).

    cum causal: Inasmuch as one [part] could not bring help to the other, the two parts of the army were fleeing.

    No indicative version would work here logically, as there is far too much cause and effect involved in the thought.

4. Cum intrā vallum nostrī [versō], sē ex castrīs ēiēcit Pompēius.

    Cum ... versārentur: imperfect subjunctive (secondary sequence).

    cum causal: Inasmuch as our men were already moving about within the rampart, Pompey rushed from the camp.

    Again, no indicative version would work here logically, as there is far too much cause and effect involved in the thought.

5. Cotīdiānīs proeliīs cum Germānīs Gallī contendunt, cum aut suīs fīnibus eōs [prohibeō] aut ipsī in eōrum fīnibus bellum [gerō].

cum ... prohibent aut ... gerunt: present indicative (primary sequence).

Indicative is the only option here, as Caesar discusses repeated and customary action. One may try present subjunctives, but to what twists of logic would we have to resort in order to force the thought into a temporal, causal, or adversative clause?

What Caesar Actually Wrote (p. 209)

Translation

Labienus followed him [Pompey] and, as he disparaged Caesar's forces, he heaped up Pompey's plan with the greatest praises: "Do not," he says, "reckon, O Pompey, that this is the army that conquered Gaul and Germany. I was present at all the battles, nor do I talk about an unknown thing recklessly. A very small part of that army survives; the large part [*majority*] has perished, [that] which was necessary [i.e., had] to happen in so many battles; disease of the autumn [time] destroyed many in Italy; many departed for home; many were left on the continent [i.e., on the mainland]. Or did you not hear from those who for the sake of health remained [behind], that new cohorts [*units*] were assembled at Brundisium? These forces, which you see, were reconstituted from the levies of those years in nearer Gaul, and very many [of them] are from the colonies beyond the Po river. And besides, what strength [literally, "of strength"] there was, perished in the two Dyrrachine battles [i.e., battles at Dyrrachium]." After he had said these things in the council, he took an oath that, unless [as] a victor, he would not return to camp, and he urged all the other [men] that they do the same. Praising this thing, Pompey swore the same thing; nor indeed of all the others was there anyone who hesitated to take the oath. When these things had been done in the council, it was departed with great hope and joy of all [*they all departed with great hope and joy*], and already they were anticipating victory in [their] imagination, because concerning so great a matter and by so experienced a commander nothing appeared to be affirmed in vain [i.e., the matter was too important and Pompey was too experienced a commander to affirm Labienus's pronouncements unless he was absolutely sure about the outcome].

After Reading What Caesar Wrote

Thinking about How Caesar Writes (p. 210)

1. In presenting Labienus's speech to Pompey's military council, Caesar switches from secondary (past tense) sequence to primary (present tense) sequence, and presents Labienus's argument in direct speech. What rhetorical effect do these choices have? Please explain.

   Points to consider: Direct speech is always more dramatic than indirect speech. The present tense is more dramatic than the past tense. Caesar loathes Labienus in proportion as he once trusted and relied on him. Labienus's speech represents a dramatic high point in the narrative. Caesar uses direct speech in the present tense to give that drama maximum rhetorical impact.

2. Why does Labienus interrogate Pompey directly? Does Labienus expect Pompey to answer his questions? Why or why not? Why are such questions where the answer is obvious often so persuasive?

   Points to consider: Labienus's questions are rhetorical. He does not expect Pompey to answer. The answers to rhetorical questions are supposed to be obvious, which is why they do not require an answer. Their rhetorical effectiveness lies in the fact that listeners will answer the questions in their own minds, thus making them complicit in the speakers' logic. The speaker, in other words, uses questions in an attempt to compel the listeners' logic to conform to his own logic because it is difficult to hear such questions without answering them the way the speaker intends.

3. Please provide evidence from Caesar to support the argument that Labienus was a braggart and a sycophant.

   Specific evidence of sycophancy: *cum . . . Pompēī consilium summīs laudibus efferret* (lines 1–2). Why does Labienus praise Pompey's plan? To ingratiate himself. Note also the superlative *summīs*.

   Specific evidence of bragging: *omnibus interfuī proeliīs* (line 4). Was Labienus really present at every single battle? Highly doubtful!

   General points to consider: Praising Pompey and disparaging Caesar both serve to build up Pompey. This represents sycophancy. Exaggerating one's role in Caesar's conquests represents bragging. Swearing not to return at all to camp unless victorious is also a rather bold statement, and, in the end, mere empty bragging, as all these oath-takers ended up running for their lives!

4. What statements in this passage would have seemed especially ironic after the battle? Why? Please explain.

> Irony: Because we know how things turned out (Pompey lost and everyone ran away), these proud statements described in the present tense contradict completely what readers know took place. Irony in general derives from statements that say one thing, but mean something else. This ironic description derives from letting the historical actors make their proud claims even though the historical record says something else. Caesar thus invites his readers to enjoy narrative irony at the expense of these hapless and ignorant speakers. This device too would serve to draw readers into Caesar's corner, as most readers prefer to be in the know and on the winning side!

Thinking about What You Read (p. 210)

These are open-ended questions, so answers can and should vary. Students should be encouraged both to use evidence from the text and to think more broadly about the issues raised, especially through any comparisons they might be able to make to analagous historical or even contemporary situations. Our answers are by no means exhaustive.

1. If you had been Labienus, how might you have defended yourself against Caesar's portrait?

   > One might argue that Caesar distorts what Labienus claimed. Did Labienus really claim as much credit as Caesar suggests? Also, perhaps Labienus had evidence to support his claims about how little of Caesar's original army remained intact. We cannot know, as Labienus's actual words do not survive. We have only Caesar's representation. Students should be encouraged to examine Caesar's representation of Labienus very closely, and ask how Caesar might have chosen to distort Labienus's words and deeds.

2. Why do people swear oaths? Why are oaths generally considered more powerful and sacred than promises? In what situations and in what professions are oaths frequently required? Why?

   > When human beings make an oath, especially in antiquity, they put themselves under an obligation to a god (especially Jupiter, guardian of oaths) whose job it was to punish liars. Atheists have existed in all ages, but most people at most times, with or without religion, recognize a solemn oath as more binding than a simple promise or statement of intent. We still require oaths of presidents, police (who are "sworn officers"), witnesses in court, those who intend to marry. The list is long.

3. Can oaths be used to motivate people? An army? A team? Please explain.

   People who have put themselves under a sacred and solemn oath have more motivation to fulfill their promises than those who have not. If they fail, they break their oaths, and thus leave themselves open to punishment by gods, public opinion, and the law.

4. If we fail to tell the truth in a court of law, we can be sent to prison. Why do we punish perjury so severely?

   Punishing perjury helps societies preserve the effectiveness of a solemn oath. Lying has consequences.

5. Labienus and Pompey lost the battle of Pharsalus against Caesar, but both escaped afterward. Did they perjure themselves? Please explain.

   Opinions will vary. Some may argue that Labienus and Pompey promised to die in battle. They lied because they lived, and ran away. Of course, this is what Caesar wants his readers to conclude. Labienus and Pompey did not surrender to Caesar and seek his clemency. Instead, they ran away to regroup and fight again. In this sense, they remained true to their oaths.

LESSON XXIII

Caesar Routs the Pompeians

Dē Bellō Cīvīlī 3.95

Now It's Your Turn (pp. 214–215)

Translate the following pairs of sentences. To what part of speech do the underlined forms belong? How do the underlined forms contribute to the logic of the sentence? How do the first and second sentence of each pair compare to each other? How did the change affect the meaning?

1. Mīlitēs cohortātus est, <u>ut</u> castra oppugnārent.
   Mīlitēs cohortātus est, <u>cum</u> castra oppugnārent.

   He urged the soldiers <u>that</u> they should storm the camp [i.e., <u>to</u> storm the camp].

   He urged the soldiers <u>when</u> they were storming the camp.

   General points to consider: both *ut* and *cum* serve in these examples as subordinating conjunctions. They establish the relationship of the subordinated thought to the main thought. Someone urged the soldiers, but for what purpose or when hangs on the conjunction. The substitution of just one word changes the meaning dramatically.

2. Castra ā cohortibus industriē dēfendēbantur, multō <u>etiam</u> ācrius ā barbarīs auxiliīs.
   Castra ā cohortibus industriē dēfendēbantur; <u>sed</u> multō ācrius ā barbarīs auxiliīs.

   The camp was defended vigorously by the cohorts, <u>and even</u> much more vehemently by the barbarian allies.

   The camp was defended vigorously by the cohorts, <u>but</u> much more vehemently by the barbarian allies.

   General points to consider: Both *etiam* and *sed* are conjunctions, the former associative, the latter dissociative. Both versions of the sentence contrast the greater vigor of the allies in defending the camp, but the first (Caesar's choice) does so more subtly and ironically by *adding* the barbarian effort to the Roman effort as opposed to simply contrasting the two through *sed*.

3. <u>Magis</u> dē reliquā fugā <u>quam</u> dē castrōrum dēfensiōne cōgitābant.
   <u>Et</u> dē reliquā fugā <u>et</u> dē castrōrum dēfensiōne cōgitābant.

   <u>More</u> concerning the remaining flight <u>than</u> concerning defense of the camp they were thinking.

   <u>Both</u> concerning the remaining flight <u>and</u> concerning defense of the camp they were thinking.

   General points to consider: Both *magis . . . quam* and *et . . . et* are coordinating conjunctions, but what a difference the choice between the two makes! In the first, we see which thought is subordinated to the other. They may think about both defense and escape, but escape is uppermost in their minds. In the second version, they think about both equally. The first represents panic; the second could represent a strategic retreat.

4. <u>Neque</u> vērō diūtius multitūdinem tēlōrum sustinēre potuērunt, <u>sed</u> confectī vulneribus locum relīquērunt.
   <u>Et</u> vērō diūtius multitūdinem tēlōrum sustinēre nōn potuērunt <u>et</u> confectī vulneribus locum relīquērunt.

   <u>Neither</u> indeed could they any longer withstand the great number of the missiles, <u>but</u>, worn out by wounds, they abandoned the place.

   They <u>both</u> could indeed not withstand the great number of the missiles any longer, <u>and</u>, worn out by wounds, they abandoned the place.

   General points to consider: *neque . . . sed* and *et . . . et* are both coordinating conjunctions, but the former incorporates dissociative contrast as well. The latter is actually not very good Latin, but we have sacrificed Latinity for the sake of illustration. Caesar, who chose the former, was, of course, a master prose stylist. The *neque* looks both back (to a previous thought) and forward to what is about to be stated. In combination with *sed*, it coordinates two closely related thoughts, but the dissociative meaning of *sed* lets us know that what is joined to the first part of the sentence took place in constrast to or in spite of that first part of the sentence. The soldiers could not withstand the great number of weapons. In spite of their efforts, they abandoned the place worn out by wounds. By using *sed*, Caesar implies that these men had done something valiant in despite of their wounds, despite the hail of missiles. This becomes clearer when we look at the coordination of the two thoughts with *et . . . et*. The soldiers could both no longer withstand the hail of missiles and, worn out by wounds, they abandoned the place. This is logical and descriptive, but it would fail to add rhetorical tension by way of contrast. Points of view are shaped through such small but crucial markers that we too often take for granted!

Stopping for Some Practice (pp. 219–220)

Translate each of the following sentences, identify the underlined word's part of speech, discuss any syntactical considerations (e.g., on mood), and discuss how the word contributes to the construction of the thought, idea, or argument conveyed by the sentence as a whole. For number three, discuss the impact that the absence of a conjunction has on the rest of the sentence.

1. Parvulae causae <u>vel</u> falsae suspīciōnis <u>vel</u> terrōris repentīnī <u>vel</u> obiectae religiōnis magna dētrīmenta saepe inferunt.

    Small causes <u>either</u> of false worry <u>or</u> of sudden terror <u>or</u> of religion [that has] occurred [i.e., religious issues that complicate present plans] often bring great harms.

    General points to consider: *vel* is a dissociative conjunction that appears here in polysyndeton. Its repetitive occurrence serves to underscore just how many small causes there are in war that can have serious consequences.

2. Parvulae causae <u>et</u> falsae suspīciōnis <u>et</u> terrōris repentīnī <u>et</u> obiectae religiōnis magna dētrīmenta saepe inferunt.

    Small causes <u>both</u> of false worry <u>and</u> of sudden terror <u>and</u> of religion [that has] occurred [i.e., religious issues that complicate present plans] often bring great harms.

    General points to consider: *et* is an associative conjunction that connects all thoughts. It appears here in polysyndeton. The implication in this version is that all these small causes together bring on serious consequences.

3. Parvulae causae terrōris repentīnī, falsae suspīciōnis, obiectae religiōnis magna dētrīmenta saepe inferunt.

    Small causes of false suspicion, of sudden worry, of religion [that has] occurred [i.e., religious issues that complicate present plans] often bring great harms.

    General points to consider: in this version we observe asyndeton. There are no conjunctions. We must supply what makes sense on our own. One might ask students which would make more sense, *vel* or *et*. *Vel*, Caesar's choice, underscores just how many small causes of disaster lurk in battle. *Et* is less logical. Asyndeton itself would likely better suit a passage in which many things were occurring at the same time, and the writer sought to emphasize an abrupt barrage.

4. <u>At</u> hostēs, <u>etiam</u> in extrēmā spē salūtis, tantam virtūtem praestitērunt <u>ut</u>, <u>cum</u> prīmī eōrum cecidissent, proximī iacentibus insisterent <u>atque</u> ex eōrum corporibus pugnārent.

> <u>But</u> the enemy, <u>and even</u> in the last [desperate] hope of safety, displayed such great manliness <u>that,</u> <u>when</u> the first of their men had fallen, the next men were standing on those lying [dead on the ground] <u>and</u> from [atop] their bodies were fighting.

> General points to consider: this relatively short sentence illustrates a number of conjunctions working in tandem to guide readers from one thought to the next and to indicate the logical relationships between the thoughts, in order to build a larger picture. *At* serves to contrast this sentence with the sentence that preceded it. *Etiam* serves to emphasize under what conditions the enemy displayed such great manliness. *Ut* introduces the result of that display. *Cum* tells us when the result took place (or under what further conditions), while the *atque* serves to coordinate two actions so we can understand how these two simultaneous actions combined to produce the result introduced by *ut*. A relatively simple sentence, but a beautifully logical one!

WHAT CAESAR ACTUALLY WROTE (P. 221)

Translation

Caesar, reckoning that it was beneficial that no room be granted to the terrified Pompeians [who had been] forced from their flight within the rampart, urged his soldiers that they should make use of the benefit of the opportunity and seize the camp. And they [*who*], although tired from the great heat (for the thing had been dragged out till noon), nevertheless prepared in mind for every effort, obeyed the command. The camp was vigorously defended by the cohorts that had been left there as a guard, and even more vehemently [was being defended] by the Thracian and barbarian allies. For the soldiers who [*which soldiers*] had fled from the battle line, both terrified in mind and worn out by weariness—very many weapons and military standards having been lost—were thinking more about the rest of their escape than about the defense of their camp. Nor indeed could [those], who had taken a stand in the rampart, any longer withstand the great number of missiles, but, worn out by wounds, they abandoned the place, and immediately all men, having relied both on the centurions and tribunes of the soldiers as leaders, fled toward the very high mountains, which were near to the camp.

After Reading What Caesar Wrote

Thinking about How Caesar Writes (p. 222)

1. Caesar comments on the physical condition of his troops as well as on their mental readiness. He also comments on his opponents' physical condition and their mental readiness. How does Caesar construct the contrast between body and mind within each description? How does Caesar guide the reader in making comparisons between the two assessments? How does the structure of each assessment contribute to the formation of the comparison and/or help the reader in seeing points of comparison?

    > General points to consider: Caesar's troops were tired, but mentally prepared for greater effort. They thus carried on in spite of their exhaustion. Pompey's troops were also very tired, but were not as mentally prepared (one recalls the overconfidence that Caesar described in the previous passage). They were thus unable to continue their resistance, and turned to flight—another sign of their mental unreadiness. Students should look for conjunctions and discuss how these conjunctions set up the contrast between physical and mental states. For example, in the second sentence we find *etsī*, *nam*, and *tamen*, which Caesar uses to build a picture of his own men. In the third sentence Caesar turns to the camps, toward which he had urged his men. In it, we find *etiam*, which helps build a picture within that sentence. The fourth sentence, introduced by *nam*, provides further explanation for the previous thought. Further elaboration is provided by *et* and *magis . . . quam. Neque, sed, –que . . . –que* guide our thought through the final sentence. Students should be encouraged to comment on what each such word contributes to the structure and logic of Caesar's arguement.

2. Identify each participle in the passage you just read, and translate it literally. After translating it literally, decide whether it could also be translated as a subordinate clause, and, if your answer is yes, please translate the participle (together with whatever other words you require from the sentence) as a subordinate clause.

    > *Caesar . . . existimāns* (lines 1–2): present active nominative singular masculine participle in agreement with the subject *Caesar* in secondary sequence. Literal translation: "Caesar, reckoning," etc. More idiomatic English translation as a subordinate clause: "Caesar, who reckoned," etc.
    >
    > *Pompēiānīs . . . compulsīs* (line 1): perfect passive dative plural masculine participle in agreement with the indirect object *Pompēiānīs* in secondary sequence. Literal translation: "to the Pompeians forced," etc. More idiomatic English translation as a subordinate clause: "to the Pompeians who had been forced," etc.

Pompēiānīs . . . perterritīs (lines 1–2): perfect passive dative plural masculine participle in agreement with the indirect object *Pompēiānīs* in secondary sequence. Literal translation: "to the terrified Pompeians," etc. In this instance, translation as a simple adjective works well, although one could also translate as a subordinate clause: "to the Pompeians, who had been terrified," etc.

Caesar . . . cohortātus est (lines 1–2): perfect active nominative masculine singular participle in agreement with the subject *Caesar*, used in the compound tense of a perfect indicative deponent verb: "Caesar urged."

quae . . . erant relictae (lines 5–6): perfect passive nominative feminine plural participle in agreement with the subject *quae*, used in the compound tense of a pluperfect indicative passive: "which had been left."

mīlitēs . . . confectī (line 8): perfect passive nominative plural masculine participle in agreement with the subject *mīlitēs* in secondary sequence. Literal translation: "the soldiers, worn out," etc. One may also well translate as a subordinate clause: "the soldiers, who had been worn out," etc.

missīs . . . armīs signīsque (lines 8–9): perfect ablative plural masculine participle in agreement with *missīs* in an ablative absolute construction in secondary sequence. Literal translation: "weapons and standards having been lost," etc. One may also well translate as a subordinate clause: "beause weapons and standards had been lost," etc.

mīlitēs . . . confectī (line 8): perfect passive nominative plural masculine participle in agreement with the subject *mīlitēs* in secondary sequence. Literal translation: "the soldiers, worn out" etc. One may also well translate as a subordinate clause: "the soldiers, who had been worn out," etc.

[*mīlitēs*] *. . . ūsī* (line 12): perfect passive nominative plural masculine participle in agreement with the subject *mīlitēs* in secondary sequence. Literal translation: "the soldiers, having used," etc. One may also well translate as a subordinate clause: "the soldiers, who had made use of," etc.

Thinking about What You Read (p. 222)

These are open-ended questions, so answers can and should vary. Students should be encouraged both to use evidence from the text and to think more broadly about the issues raised, especially through any comparisons they might be able to make to analagous historical or even contemporary situations. Our answers are by no means exhaustive.

1. Why does Caesar mention the ethnicity of those who best defended Pompey's camp? What does this imply about Roman allies? About Pompey's Roman troops? About the scale of Rome's civil war?

   Because (in Caesar's representation), Pompey's non-Roman allies fight harder than Pompey's Roman troops, Caesar implies that Pompey's Roman troops are not fully committed to Pompey's cause. Roman allies, even those allied with Caesar's enemies, are loyal and effective fighting men. We also can see that Rome's civil war involves everyone in the Roman world, not just Roman citizens. The scale of the war is as vast as the empire.

2. What do you think some of the obstacles were that Roman generals faced in coordinating multiethnic forces? What dangers do you think may have increased in a time of civil war?

   Multiethnic forces require more coordination in terms of language as well as other accommodations to keep them on board. There is always a danger that they may find a better deal with the other side, and then switch sides, as they may not be as fully vested in the interests of one side or another as native forces. And in a civil war, all loyalties often waver.

3. Caesar once again stresses the importance of the soldiers' mental attitude or morale. Do you think that Caesar is right or wrong to emphasize this? Please explain.

   Morale is a crucial factor for any fighting force. Caesar is correct to focus on morale. Students should be encouraged to think of instances in their own experience where morale and attitude made a difference. Student athletes and theater students, in particular, may be able to speak about this from their personal experience.

4. Do you think that an army's morale matters as much for a modern army as it did for a Roman army? Please explain.

   The answer depends on what army and in what kind of war. Do the soldiers sit somewhere at home, shooting missiles or drones remotely, or are the soldiers part of a force in enemy territory? Soldiers in the field require esprit de corps for the efficient operation of their unit and to ensure mutual aid and cooperation. But even soldiers safe at home who participate remotely will likely perform better if they believe in the mission. One of the greatest security breaches in American history resulted from a soldier's disaffection with the way the United States was conducting the war in Iraq. This soldier (Bradley Manning) collected a huge trove of sensitive documents and released them to WikiLeaks. In Vietnam, disaffected soldiers began shooting their own commanders. Morale and belief in the mission matter.

LESSON XXIV

Caesar Visits Pompey's Camp but Pompey Escapes

Dē Bellō Cīvīlī 3.96

Now It's Your Turn (pp. 224–225)

Translate each sentence, and parse (i.e., identify the case and the reason[s] for the case of) the underlined adjective. If it is a special kind of adjective (e.g., a participle), please state what that is, and please comment too on any other interesting or peculiar aspects of the syntax.

1. Exercituī Caesaris semper <u>omnia</u> dēfuērunt.

   <u>All things</u> were lacking for Caesar's army. [I.e., Caesar's army lacked all necessary supplies.]

   omnia: nominative neuter plural; subject.

2. Intrā vallum <u>nostrī</u> versābantur.

   <u>Our men</u> were wandering about within the rampart.

   nostrī: nominative masculine plural; subject.

3. Scūtum ab <u>novissimīs</u> ūnī mīlitī dētrāctum est.

   A shield was taken away from one soldier by <u>the men at the end</u> [literally, "<u>most recent</u>," i.e., "<u>last</u>," <u>men</u>].

   novissimīs: ablative masculine plural; ablative of agent.

4. Ea facilia ex <u>difficillimīs</u> animī magnitūdō redēgerat.

   Greatness of spirit had from <u>very difficult matters</u> [i.e., <u>a very difficult state of affairs</u>] rendered these things easy.

   difficillimīs: ablative neuter plural; with preposition *ex*.

5. <u>Paucōs suōs</u> ex fugā Pompēius nactus est.

   Pompey found <u>a few of his own</u> men during his flight.

   Paucōs suōs: accusative maculine plural; direct object.

Stopping for Some Practice (pp. 231–232)

Translate each sentence, identify the adjective being used as a substantive, and explain its syntax.

1. Suōs urgērī dicēbant.

    The said that their men were being pressed.

    Adjective used substantively: *suōs*; accusative masculine plural; subject of the infinitive *urgērī* in indirect statement dependent on *dicēbant*.

2. Reliquī erant tardiōrēs.

    The other men were slower.

    Adjective used substantively: *reliquī*; nominative masculine plural; subject.

3. Ab parvulīs dūritiae student Germānī.

    From the time when they are small children [literally, from little ones] the Germans are eager for toughness.

    Adjective used substantively: *parvulīs*; ablative masculine plural with the preposition *ab*.

4. Pompēius āmissa restituisse vidētur.

    Pompey seems to have restored the things that had been lost.

    Adjective used substantively: *āmissa*; accusative neuter plural; direct object of the infinitive *restituisse*, but used as the equivalent of a subordinate clause.

5. Annōs nōnnullī vīcēnōs in disciplīnā permanent.

    Many remain in study for twenty years.

    Adjective used substantively: *nōnnullī*; nominative masculine plural; subject.

What Caesar Actually Wrote (pp. 227, 229, 231)

Translation

In the camp of Pompey it was possible to see bowers [that had been] built, a large amount [*weight*] of silver [i.e., silverplate] laid out, tents strewn over with fresh sod, and also the tents of Lucius Lentulus and many others garlanded with ivy, and many other things besides, which would signify too great luxury and confidence in victory, with the result that easily it could be reckoned that they had feared not at all concerning the outcome of that day, [i.e., those] who were searching out not necessary pleasures.

But they used to set out [as an accusation] Caesar's luxury before [his] most wretched and long-suffering army, for whom all things for necessary use had always been lacking [i.e., who had always lacked all necessities]. Pompey, already while our men were wandering about within the rampart, having found a horse—the insignia of his command having been removed—rushed from the decuman gate [i.e., the main gate farthest from the enemy], and immediately—his horse having been spurred—hastened toward Larissa. Nor did he stop there, but with the same haste, having found a few of his own men—a night journey not having been omitted—with an escort of thirty cavalry, arrived at the sea, and boarded a grain ship, often, as it was reported, lamenting that so great a trust [in others] had deceived him, with the result that, by means of which class of men he had expected victory, by means of that [class]—the beginning of flight having been made—he appeared almost to have been betrayed.

After Reading What Caesar Wrote

Thinking about How Caesar Writes (p. 232)

1. What is the rhetorical effect of the asyndeton in the first sentence of this passage?

    Points to consider: The asyndeton reproduces the effect of a darting eye. Our gaze is directed to one luxury after another in succession without interruption. The asyndeton serves to speed up the narrative and give the reader a sense of the sudden onslaught of visual details that greeted Caesar's conquering soldiers.

2. What is the rhetorical effect of the hyperbaton in the third sentence? (Think about everything that comes between subject and verb.)

    Points to consider: The sentence begins with the subject *Pompēius*, and ends with then main verb *contendit*. In between, we accompany the subject Pompey on his flight. The hyperbaton serves to bring us along (rhetorically) for the long ride.

3. In the last sentence, we have an example of indirect speech introduced by a participle (*querēns*). How do we determine that *opīniōnem* and not *sē* is the accusative subject of the infinitive *fefellisse*?

> Points to consider: Context. Would it make sense that Pompey would complain about how he deceived the trust placed in himself? Caesar portrays Pompey as spoiled. Instead, Pompey complains about how the trust (that he had placed in others) deceived him.

4. This passage is neatly balanced between the actions of the Pompeians in the first two sentences and the actions of Pompey in the third and fourth sentences. How does Caesar use the contrast between the followers and leader to build a composite portrait of his opponents? Caesar draws other comparisons too: what constrasts do you think Caesar hopes his readers will observe between the conduct, on the one hand, of the Pompeians and their leader, and, on the other, of Caesar's soldiers and their leader? Please explain.

> Points to consider: The Pompeians were self-indulgent. Pompey was, in the end (at least in Caesar's devastating portrait), a coward who blamed his magnanimous trust in others for his debacle. In the end, both followers and leaders appear both self-indulgent and self-deceiving. By way of contrast, Caesar and his army were tough. They had lacked creature comforts and necessary supplies. They were thus more virtuous (because more manly), and so (at least this is what Caesar implies) deserved their victory.

Thinking about What You Read (p. 232)

These are open-ended questions, so answers can and should vary. Students should be encouraged both to use evidence from the text and to think more broadly about the issues raised, especially through any comparisons they might be able to make to analagous historical or even contemporary situations. Our answers are by no means exhaustive.

1. If you did not know that Pompey was one of the greatest generals and statesmen of his age, that Caesar was the one who had rebelled against the legitimate goverment, what conclusion would you draw about Pompey and his followers? How does Caesar's portrait compare with these historical facts?

> Caesar's portrait of Pompey's camp makes it appear that Pompey's camp contained a spoiled and selfish elite, while Caesar's army was, on the other hand, composed of true Romans, men who lacked basics, but who fought for a noble cause: Caesar's. Rome's ruling class was indeed spoiled and rich. Caesar's portrait is not unfair. On the other hand, the ruling class, not the Romans who followed Caesar, constituted the legally legitimate government, no matter how spoiled they may have been.

2. On the other hand, we have Cicero's private correspondence (not meant for publication) which tends to confirm Caesar's unflattering portrait of Pompey and his followers. Does this mean that Caesar's portrait was true? Is it possible for a great general and statesman to have been as petty and arrogant as Caesar describes him? Can you think of any more modern examples of politicians and generals who have won great victories, but who were, in private, petty and arrogant? Please explain.

   Caesar's portrait is likely not untrue. On the other hand, is it fair to judge Pompey's side from behind the scenes, but Caesar's side only from the perspective of his public victory? It is not an even-handed comparison. And many public figures have more than one face. It should not surprise us that great men could also be petty and vain. We lack Pompey's representation of the events. As to modern examples, it should be interesting to observe whom students might name and for what reasons.

3. How do we reconcile such contradictions between public and private conduct? Why is it generally an effective rhetorical strategy to accuse one's political and military opponents of such vices as arrogance, self-indulgence, and luxurious living? Can you think of any modern instances where any or all of these categories have been alleged by one leader against another? Is it possible to use just one or two of these categories? How would using just one or two of the categories change the force of the argument? Please explain. Can you think of examples?

   Private conduct is thought to reflect on how a public figure might conduct public business as well. Can soldiers, for example, trust a general who is himself afraid to enter battle? Politicians (and blackmailers) famously try to "dig up dirt" on their opponents to tarnish their reputations (or extort money). Generals too depend on their reputation to command the respect of their troops. Reputation matters. Anything that undermines confidence in a general (as contradictions between public image and private conduct tend to do) can reduce his effectiveness.

4. Caesar does not state explicitly that Pompey and those around him broke their oaths to return victorious or not to return at all. Do you, however, think that his readers would have remembered those oaths? Are there any hints in the Latin text that Caesar wanted his readers to remember those oaths? Please cite the Latin, and explain your thinking.

   Caesar mentions that Pompey removed the insignia of his command (*dētractīs insignibus imperātōris*, line 10). Pompey thus abandons his command and the troops who had sworn allegiance to him. Moreover, Pompey complains that he was betrayed by the very people in whom he had placed his trust, and who were the first to run away (*querēns tantum sē opīniōnem fefellisse, ut,*

ā quō genere hominum victōriam spērāsset, ab eō initiō fugae factō paene prōditus vidērētur, lines 14–16). Which "sort of men" (*genere hominum*, line 15) had Pompey counted on? He probably counted on the ones who had vowed to fight until the death. Caesar likely brings readers back to a recollection of their overconfident oaths through such suggestions and echoes.

CONCLUSION & POST-READING

REFLECTIONS ON CAESAR BY LATER AUTHORS

Valerius Maximus *Facta et Dicta Memorābilia*
(*Memorable Deeds and Sayings*) 4.5.6
Plutarch *Life of Caesar* 60–69

WHAT VALERIUS MAXIMUS WROTE ABOUT CAESAR: A MODEST DEATH

Translation

What outstanding personal modesty had also been [present] in Gaius [Julius] Caesar was both often apparent and his last day demonstrated: for, having been wounded by the very many daggers of the parricides, at that very time, during which the divine soul was separated from mortal body, not even by twenty-three wounds could he be deterred, but that he obeyed [the dictates of] personal modesty, if indeed [which of course he did] with either hand [i.e., with both hands] he let drop his toga, so that the lower part of his body might fall covered. In this manner human beings do not die, but rather immortal gods return to their temples.

AFTER READING WHAT VALERIUS MAXIMUS WROTE (P. 237)

1. Valerius Maximus uses a number of words that imply either human or divine status. What are those words?

    Some words indicating divinity: *dīvīnus, dī immortālēs, sēdēs.*

    Some words indicating human status: *mortālis, corpus, hominēs*

2. What parts of Caesar were human? What part of him became divine?

   Mortal: *corpus*. This is not problematic, as bodies are obviously mortal.

   Immortal: *spīritus*. This word is not easy. It originally meant "breath" in Latin. Bodies that breathe are alive. When breath leaves, the body is dead. But when did the word acquire the meaning of "soul," particularly "immortal soul"? Valerius's usage represents a step in the history of this conception.

3. How does Caesar's death, which demonstrated *verēcundia*, also help elevate Caesar above (or, in Valerius's view, demonstrate his more than) merely human status?

   Some points to consider: The Romans placed great importance on how one behaved in the moment of one's death, as it was in such moments that one's true character was revealed. We thus have many stories of the final acts and last words of famous Romans, and Caesar's assassination certainly ranks among the most famous of them all. Most human beings would likely flinch or try to run away under a barrage of daggers. Not Caesar. His dignified exit from life and the mortal world signal to Valerius a divine nature. And we may recall also that Valerius wrote almost a century after Caesar had been declared a god by the Senate. In Valerius's mind, because his task is to describe historical facts, he makes the best sense of the record that he can.

What Plutarch Wrote:
Resentment, Omens, and Assassination

Plutarch *Life of Caesar* 60–69

After Reading What Plutarch Wrote:
Did It Have to Happen This Way? (p. 241)

1. According to Plutarch, why were Caesar's senatorial colleagues so angry with him?

   Points to consider: §60: Caesar's desire for royal power, general resentment and hatred. Jealously of his extravagant honors, Caesar's disrespect for republican values (his failure to rise from his seat). §61: Insult to the tribunes Flavius and Marulla during the Lupercalia (who pulled the crown off his statue). In other words, senatorial colleagues especially (but also people more generally) resented Caesar's aspirations for unconstitutional royal, as opposed to constitutional republican, authority.

2. Why do you think Caesar failed to pay attention to those who tried to warn him? Please explain.

   Answers will likely vary, but students should be encouraged to cite the text in justifying their responses.

3. Among the many aims of the framers of the US Constitution, one important goal was to design a framework for government that would make it very difficult for an ambitious politician or general to seize dictatorial control of the entire government on the model of Caesar. What principles of the US Constitution do you think might be especially effective in preventing someone like Caesar from overthrowing this modern republic? Please explain, and, if you can, please support your response with evidence from your readings in this book.

   This is an open-ended question. Answers will—and certainly should—vary.

   NB: The following website on the US Constitution is a good resource:

   http://www.archives.gov/exhibits/charters/constitution.html

THE UNADAPTED LATIN PASSAGES

PRE-CAESAR READING

Sallust *Bellum Catilīnae* 54

What Sallust Actually Wrote (p. 4)

[*Bellum Catilīnae* 54] Igitur eīs genus, aetās, ēloquentia prope aequālia fuēre, magnitūdō animī pār, item glōria, sed alia aliī. Caesar beneficiīs ac mūnificentiā magnus habēbātur, integritāte vītae Cato. Ille mānsuētūdine et
5 misericordiā clārus factus, huic sevēritās dignitātem addiderat . . . In alterō miserīs perfugium erat, in alterō malīs perniciēs. Illīus facilitās, huius cōnstantia laudābātur.

LESSON I

CAESAR DISCUSSES THE GAULS

Dē Bellō Gallicō 1.1

WHAT CAESAR ACTUALLY WROTE (P. 10)

[*DBG* 1.1] Gallia est omnis dīvīsa in partēs trēs, quārum ūnam incolunt Belgae, aliam Aquītānī, tertiam quī ipsōrum linguā Celtae, nostrā Gallī appellantur. Hī omnēs linguā, īnstitūtīs, lēgibus inter sē differunt. Gallōs ab
5 Aquītānīs Garumna flūmen, ā Belgīs Matrona et Sēquana dīvidit. Hōrum omnium fortissimī sunt Belgae, proptereā quod ā cultū atque hūmānitāte Prōvinciae longissimē absunt, minimēque saepe ad eōs mercātōrēs veniunt atque ea quae ad effēminandōs animōs pertinent
10 important. Proximī sunt Germānīs, quī trans Rhēnum incolunt, quibuscum continenter bellum gerunt.

LESSON II

Caesar Encounters the Nervii

Dē Bellō Gallicō 2.15.5–12

What Caesar Actually Wrote (p. 17)

[*DBG* 2.15.5–12] Eōrum fīnēs Nerviī attingēbant. Quōrum dē nātūrā mōribusque Caesar cum quaereret, sīc reperiēbat: nullum esse aditum ad eōs mercātōribus; nihil patī vīnī reliquārumque rērum ad luxuriam
5 pertinentium inferrī, quod hīs rēbus relanguescere animōs eōrum et remittī virtūtem existimārent; esse hominēs ferōs magnaeque virtūtis; increpitāre atque incūsāre reliquōs Belgās, quī sē populō Rōmānō dēdidissent patriamque virtūtem prōiēcissent; confirmāre
10 sēsē neque lēgātōs missūrōs neque ullam condiciōnem pācis acceptūrōs.

LESSON III

THE BATTLE BEGINS, PART 1
Dē Bellō Gallicō 2.20.1–9

WHAT CAESAR ACTUALLY WROTE (P. 28)

[*DBG* 2.20.1–9] Caesarī omnia ūnō tempore erant agenda: vexillum prōpōnendum, quod erat insigne, cum ad arma concurrī oportēret; ab opere revocandī mīlitēs; quī paulō longius aggeris petendī causā prōcesserant arcessendī;
5 aciēs īnstruenda; mīlitēs cohortandī; signum tubā dandum. Quārum rērum magnam partem temporis brevitās et incursus hostium impediēbat. Hīs difficultātibus duae rēs erant subsidiō, scientia atque ūsus mīlitum, quī, superiōribus proeliīs exercitātī, sibi
10 quid fierī oportēret praescrībere poterant; et quod ab opere singulīsque legiōnibus singulōs lēgātōs Caesar discēdere nisi mūnītīs castrīs vetuerat. Hī propter propinquitātem et celeritātem hostium nihil iam Caesaris imperium expectābant, sed per sē quae vidēbantur administrābant.

LESSON IV

The Battle Begins, Part 2
Dē Bellō Gallicō 2.22.1–5

What Caesar Actually Wrote (p. 36)

[*DBG* 2.22.1–5] Īnstrūctus est exercitus magis ut locī nātūra et necessitās temporis quam ut reī mīlitāris ratiō atque ordō postulābat, cum dīversae legiōnēs aliae aliā in parte hostibus resisterent saepibusque densissimīs
5 interiectīs prōspectus impedīrētur. Neque certa subsidia collocārī neque quid in quāque parte opus esset prōvidērī neque ab ūnō omnia imperia administrārī poterant. Itaque in tantā rērum inīquitāte fortūnae quoque ēventūs variī sequēbantur.

LESSON V

The Thick of the Fight
Dē Bellō Gallicō 2.24.1–12

What Caesar Actually Wrote (p. 47)

[*DBG* 2.24.1–12] Eōdem tempore equitēs nostrī levisque armātūrae peditēs, quī cum eīs ūnā fuerant, quōs prīmō hostium impetū pulsōs dīxeram, cum sē in castra reciperent, adversīs hostibus occurrēbant ac rūrsus aliam
5   in partem fugam petēbant; et cālōnēs, quī ab decumānā portā ac summō iugō collis nostrōs victōrēs flūmen trānsīre cōnspexerant, praedandī causā ēgressī, cum respexissent et hostēs in nostrīs castrīs versārī vīdissent, praecipitēs fugae sēsē mandābant. Simul eōrum quī cum
10   impedīmentīs veniēbant clāmor fremitusque oriēbātur, aliīque aliam in partem perterritī ferēbantur. Quibus omnibus rēbus permōtī equitēs Trēverī, quōrum inter Gallōs virtūtis opīniō est singulāris, quī auxiliī causā ā cīvitāte missī ad Caesarem vēnerant, cum multitūdine
15   hostium castra [nostra] complērī, legiōnēs premī et paene circumventās tenērī, cālōnēs, equitēs, funditōrēs, Numidās dīversōs dissipātōsque in omnēs partēs fugere vīdissent, dēspērātīs nostrīs rēbus domum contendērunt: Rōmānōs pulsōs superātōsque, castrīs impedīmentīsque eōrum
20   hostēs potītōs cīvitātī renūntiāvērunt.

LESSON VI

Slowing the Onslaught
Dē Bellō Gallicō 2.25.1–14

What Caesar Actually Wrote (p. 59)

[*DBG* 2.25.1–14] Caesar ab decimae legiōnis cohortātiōne ad dextrum cornū profectus est, ubi suōs urgērī signīsque in ūnum locum collātīs duodecimae legiōnis cōnfertōs mīlitēs sibi ipsōs ad pugnam esse impedīmentō vīdit.
5 Quārtae cohortis omnēs centuriōnēs occīsī erant; signiferōque interfectō, signum āmissum erat; reliquārum cohortium omnibus ferē centuriōnibus aut vulnerātīs aut occīsīs, in hīs prīmipīlus P. Sextius Baculus, fortissimus vir, multīs gravibusque vulneribus confectus,
10 ut iam sē sustinēre nōn posset. Reliquī erant tardiōrēs et nōnnullī ab novissimīs dēsertō locō proeliō excēdēbant ac tēla vītābant. Hostēs neque ā fronte ex īnferiōre locō subeuntēs intermittere et ab utrōque latere īnstāre et rem esse in angustō vīdit, neque ūllum esse subsidium
15 quod submittī posset; scūtō ab novissimīs ūnī mīlitī dētractō, quod ipse eō sine scūtō vēnerat, in prīmam aciem prōcessit centuriōnibusque nōminātim appellātīs reliquōs cohortātus mīlitēs signa īnferre et manipulōs laxāre iussit, quō facilius gladiīs ūtī possent. Cuius
20 adventū spē illātā mīlitibus ac redintegrātō animō, cum prō sē quisque in conspectū imperātōris etiam in extrēmīs suīs rēbus operam nāvāre cuperet, paulum hostium impetus tardātus est.

LESSON VII

The Hard-won Victory

Dē Bellō Gallicō 2.27.1–10

What Caesar Actually Wrote (p. 67)

[*DBG* 2.27.1–10] Decimae legiōnis adventū tanta rērum commūtātiō est facta ut nostrī, etiam quī vulneribus confectī prōcubuissent, scūtīs innīxī proelium redintegrārent, cālōnēs perterritōs hostēs cōnspicātī etiam
5 inermēs armātīs occurrerent, equitēs vērō, ut turpitūdinem fugae virtūte dēlērent, omnibus in locīs pugnandō sē legiōnāriīs mīlitibus praeferrent. At hostēs, etiam in extrēmā spē salūtis, tantam virtūtem praestitērunt ut, cum prīmī eōrum cecidissent, proximī
10 iacentibus insisterent atque ex eōrum corporibus pugnārent; hīs dēiectīs et coacervātīs cadāveribus quī superessent ut ex tumulō tēla in nostrōs conicerent et pīla intercepta remitterent: ut nōn nēquīquam tantae virtūtis hominēs iūdicārī dēbēret ausōs esse trānsīre
15 lātissimum flūmen, ascendere altissimās rīpās, subīre inīquissimum locum; quae facilia ex difficillimīs animī magnitūdō redēgerat.

LESSON VIII

The Outcome

Dē Bellō Gallicō 2.35

What Caesar Actually Wrote (p. 74)

[*DBG* 2.35] Hīs rēbus gestīs Gallia omnis pācāta est. Tanta hūius bellī ad barbarōs opīniō perlāta est utī ab eīs nātiōnibus quae trāns Rhēnum incolerent lēgātī ad Caesarem mitterentur, quī sē obsidēs datūrōs, imperāta
5   factūrōs pollicērentur. Quās lēgātōs Caesar, quod in Ītaliam Īllyricumque properābat, initā proximā aestāte ad sē revertī iussit. Ipse in Carnutēs, Andēs, Turonōs quaeque cīvitātēs propinquae hīs locīs erant ubi bellum gesserat, legiōnibus in hīberna dēductīs, in Ītaliam
10 profectus est. Ob eāsque rēs ex litterīs Caesaris diērum quīndecim supplicātiō dēcrēta est, quod ante id tempus accidit nūllī.

LESSON IX

THE DRUIDS OF GAUL

Dē Bellō Gallicō 6.13.4–7

WHAT CAESAR ACTUALLY WROTE (P. 82)

[*DBG* 6.13.4–7] Illī rēbus dīvīnīs intersunt, sacrificia pūblica ac prīvāta prōcūrant, religiōnēs interpretantur: ad hōs magnus adulescentium numerus disciplīnae causā concurrit, magnōque hī sunt apud eōs honōre. Nam ferē
5   dē omnibus contrōversiīs pūblicīs prīvātīsque constituunt, et, sī quod est admissum facinus, sī caedēs facta, sī dē hērēditāte, dē fīnibus contrōversia est, īdem dēcernunt, praemia poenāsque constituunt; sī quī aut prīvātus aut populus eōrum dēcrētō nōn stetit, sacrificiīs interdīcunt.
10 Haec poena apud eōs est gravissima. Quibus ita est interdictum, hī numerō impiōrum ac scelerātōrum habentur, hīs omnēs dēcēdunt, aditum sermōnemque dēfugiunt, nē quid ex contāgiōne incommodī accipiant, neque hīs petentibus iūs redditur neque honōs ullus
15 commūnicātur.

LESSON X

The Training of the Druids
Dē Bellō Gallicō 6.14.1–4

What Caesar Actually Wrote (p. 90)

[*DBG* 6.14.1–4] Druidēs ā bellō abesse cōnsuērunt neque tribūta ūnā cum reliquīs pendunt; mīlitiae vacātiōnem omniumque rērum habent immūnitātem. Tantīs excitātī praemiīs et suā sponte multī in disciplīnam
5 conveniunt et ā parentibus propinquīsque mittuntur. Magnum ibi numerum versuum ēdiscere dīcuntur. Itaque annōs nōnnullī vīcēnōs in disciplīnā permanent. Neque fās esse exīstimant ea litterīs mandāre, cum in reliquīs ferē rēbus, pūblicīs prīvātīsque ratiōnibus Graecīs
10 litterīs ūtantur. Id mihi duābus dē causīs instituisse videntur, quod neque in vulgum disciplīnam efferrī velint neque eōs, quī discunt, litterīs confīsōs minus memoriae studēre: quod ferē plērīsque accidit, ut praesidiō litterārum dīligentiam in perdiscendō ac
15 memoriam remittant.

LESSON XI

Marriage among the Gauls
Dē Bellō Gallicō 6.19.1–3

What Caesar Actually Wrote (p. 98)

[*DBG* 6.19.1–3] Virī, quantās pecūniās ab uxōribus dōtis nōmine accēpērunt, tantās ex suīs bonīs aestimātiōne factā cum dōtibus commūnicant. Hūius omnis pecūniae coniūnctim ratiō habētur frūctūsque servantur: uter
5 eōrum vītā superāvit, ad eum pars utrīusque cum frūctibus superiōrum temporum pervēnit. Virī in uxōrēs, sīcutī in līberōs, vītae necisque habent potestātem; et cum pater familiae illūstriōre locō nātus dēcessit, ēius propinquī conveniunt et, dē morte sī rēs in suspīciōnem
10 vēnit, dē uxōribus in servīlem modum quaestiōnem habent et, sī compertum est, ignī atque omnibus tormentīs excruciātās interficiunt.

LESSON XII

Politics among the Gauls

Dē Bellō Gallicō 6.20.1–3

What Caesar Actually Wrote (p. 104)

[*DBG* 6.20.1–3] Quae cīvitātēs commodius suam rem pūblicam administrāre exīstimantur, habent lēgibus sānctum, sī quis quid dē rē pūblicā ā fīnitimīs rūmōre aut fāmā accēperit, utī ad magistrātum dēferat nēve cum
5   quō aliō commūnicet, quod saepe hominēs temerāriōs atque imperītōs falsīs rūmōribus terrērī et ad facinus impellī et dē summīs rēbus cōnsilium capere cōgnitum est. Magistrātūs quae vīsa sunt occultant quaeque esse ex ūsū iūdicāvērunt multitūdinī prōdunt. Dē rē pūblicā
10 nisi per concilium loquī nōn concēditur.

LESSON XIII

THE GERMANS LIVE SIMPLY

Dē Bellō Gallicō 6.21

WHAT CAESAR ACTUALLY WROTE (P. 114)

[*DBG* 6.21] Germānī multum ab hāc consuētūdine differunt. Nam neque Druidēs habent, quī rēbus dīvīnīs praesint, neque sacrificiīs student. Deōrum numerō eōs sōlōs dūcunt, quōs cernunt et quōrum apertē opibus
5 iuvantur, Sōlem et Vulcānum et Lūnam, reliquōs nē fāmā quidem accēpērunt. Vīta omnis in vēnātiōnibus atque in studiīs reī mīlitāris consistit: ab parvulīs labōrī ac dūritiae student. Quī diūtissimē impūberēs permansērunt, maximam inter suōs ferunt laudem:
10 hōc aliī statūram, aliī vīrēs nervōsque confirmārī putant. Intrā annum vērō vīcēsimum fēminae nōtitiam habuisse in turpissimīs habent rēbus; cūius reī nulla est occultātiō, quod et prōmiscuē in flūminibus perluuntur et pellibus aut parvīs rēnōnum tegimentīs ūtuntur magnā corporis
15 parte nūdā.

LESSON XIV

Caesar Describes the German Lifestyle, Such as it May Have Been

Dē Bellō Gallicō 6.22

What Caesar Actually Wrote (p. 124)

[*DBG* 6.22] Agricultūrae nōn student, maiorque pars eōrum victūs inlacte, cāseō, carne consistit. Neque quisquam agrī modum certum aut fīnēs habet propriōs; sed magistrātūs ac principēs in annōs singulōs gentibus
5 cognātiōnibusque hominum, quī ūnā coiērunt, quantum et quō locō vīsum est agrī attribuunt atque annō post aliō transīre cōgunt. Ēius reī multās adferunt causās: nē adsiduā consuētūdine captī studium bellī gerendī agricultūrā commūtent; nē lātōs fīnēs parāre studeant,
10 potentiōrēsque humiliōrēs possessiōnibus expellant; nē accūrātius ad frīgora atque aestūs vītandōs aedificent; nē qua oriātur pecūniae cupiditās, quā ex rē factiōnēs dissēnsiōnēsque nascuntur; ut animī aequitāte plēbem contineant, cum suās quisque opēs cum potentissimīs
15 aequārī videat.

LESSON XV

THE GERMANS DO NOT MAKE GOOD NEIGHBORS BUT THEY DO TREAT GUESTS WELL

Dē Bellō Gallicō 6.23

WHAT CAESAR ACTUALLY WROTE (P. 135)

[*DBG* 6.23] Cīvitātibus maxima laus est quam lātissimē circum sē vastātīs fīnibus sōlitūdinēs habēre. Hoc proprium virtūtis existimant, expulsōs agrīs fīnitimōs cēdere, neque quemquam prope audēre consistere;
5   simul hōc sē fore tūtiōrēs arbitrantur repentīnae incursiōnis timōre sublātō. Cum bellum cīvitās aut illātum dēfendit aut infert, magistrātūs, quī eī bellō praesint, ut vītae necisque habeant potestātem, dēliguntur. In pāce nullus est commūnis magistrātus, sed principēs regiōnum
10 atque pāgōrum inter suōs iūs dīcunt contrōversiāsque minuunt. Latrōcinia nullam habent infāmiam, quae extrā fīnēs cūiusque cīvitātis fīunt, atque ea iuventūtis exercendae ac dēsidiae minuendae causā fierī praedīcant. Atque ubī quis ex principibus in conciliō dīxit sē ducem
15 fore, quī sequī velint, profiteantur. Consurgunt eī quī et causam et hominem probant suumque auxilium pollicentur atque ab multitūdine collaudantur: quī ex hīs secūtī nōn sunt, in dēsertōrum ac prōditōrum numerō dūcuntur, omniumque hīs rērum posteā fidēs dērogātur.
20 Hospitem violāre fās nōn putant; quī quācumque dē causā ad eōs venērunt, ab iniūriā prohibent, sanctōs habent, hīsque omnium domūs patent victusque commūnicātur.

Lesson XVI

Gauls and Germans Compared
Dē Bellō Gallicō 6.24

What Caesar Actually Wrote (p. 143)

[*DBG* 6.24] Ac fuit anteā tempus, cum Germānōs Gallī virtūte superārent, ultrō bella inferrent, propter hominum multitūdinem agrīque inopiam trans Rhēnum colōniās mitterent. Itaque ea quae fertilissima Germāniae sunt
5   loca circum Hercyniam silvam, quam Eratosthenī et quibusdam Graecīs fāmā nōtam esse videō, quam illī Orcyniam appellant, Volcae Tectosagēs occupāvērunt atque ibi consēdērunt; quae gens ad hoc tempus hīs sēdibus sēsē continet summamque habet iustitiae et
10 bellicae laudis opīniōnem. Nunc quod in eādem inopiā, egestāte, patientiā quā Germānī permanent, eōdem victū et cultū corporis ūtuntur; Gallīs autem prōvinciārum propinquitās et transmarīnārum rērum nōtitia multa ad cōpiam atque ūsūs largitur, paulātim
15 adsuēfactī superārī multīsque victī proeliīs nē sē quidem ipsī cum illīs virtūte comparant.

LESSON XVII

The Senate Debates Caesar

Dē Bellō Cīvīlī 1.1

What Caesar Actually Wrote (p. 155)

[*DBC* 1.1] Litterīs C. Caesaris consulibus redditīs aegrē ab hīs impetrātum est summā tribūnōrum plēbis contentiōne, ut in senātū recitārentur; ut vērō ex litterīs ad senātum referrētur, impetrārī nōn potuit. Referunt
5 consulēs dē rē pūblicā. L. Lentulus consul senātuī reīque pūblicae sē nōn dēfutūrum pollicētur, sī audacter ac fortiter sententiās dīcere velint; sīn Caesarem respiciant atque ēius grātiam sequantur, ut superiōribus fēcerint temporibus, sē sibi consilium captūrum neque senātūs
10 auctōritātī obtemperātūrum: habēre sē quoque ad Caesaris grātiam atque amīcitiam receptum. In eandem sententiam loquitur Scīpiō: Pompēiō esse in animō reī pūblicae nōn dēesse, sī senātus sequātur; sī cunctētur atque agat lēnius, nēquīquam ēius auxilium, sī posteā
15 velit, senātum implōrātūrum.

LESSON XVIII

Discussion, Debate, and a Decree against Caesar in the Senate

Dē Bellō Cīvīlī 1.2

What Caesar Actually Wrote (pp. 167–168)

[*DBC* 1.2] Haec Scīpiōnis ōrātiō, quod senātus in urbe habēbātur Pompēiusque aberat, ex ipsīus ōre Pompēī mittī vidēbātur. Dīxerat aliquis lēniōrem sententiam, ut prīmō M. Marcellus, ingressus in eam ōrātiōnem, nōn
5 oportēre ante dē eā rē ad senātum referrī, quam dīlectūs tōtā Ītaliā habitī et exercitūs cōnscrīptī essent, quō praesidiō tūtō et līberē senātus, quae vellet, dēcernere audēret; ut M. Calidius, quī cēnsēbat, ut Pompēius in suās prōvinciās proficīscerētur, nē quā esset armōrum
10 causa: timēre Caesarem ēreptīs ab eō duābus legiōnibus, nē ad ēius perīculum reservāre et retinēre eās ad urbem Pompēius vidērētur; ut M. Rūfus, quī sententiam Calidiī paucīs ferē rēbus mūtātīs sequēbātur. Hī omnēs convīciō L. Lentulī cōnsulis correptī exagitābantur. Lentulus
15 sententiam Calidiī prōnuntiātūrum sē omnīnō negāvit. Marcellus perterritus convīciīs ā suā sententiā discessit. Sīc vōcibus cōnsulis, terrōre praesentis exercitūs, minīs amīcōrum Pompēī plērīque compulsī invītī et coāctī Scīpiōnis sententiam sequuntur: utī ante certam diem
20 Caesar exercitum dīmittat; sī nōn faciat, eum adversus rem pūblicam factūrum vidērī.

LESSON XIX

Abused Tribunes and Insults to Caesar's Personal Dignity

Dē Bellō Cīvīlī 1.7

What Caesar Actually Wrote (p. 177)

[*DBC* 1.7] Quibus rēbus cognitīs Caesar apud mīlitēs contiōnātur. Omnium temporum iniūriās inimīcōrum in sē commemorat; ā quibus dēductum ac dēprāvātum Pompēium queritur invidiā atque obtrectātiōne laudis
5   suae, cūius ipse honōrī et dignitātī semper fāverit adiūtorque fuerit. Novum in rē pūblicā intrōductum exemplum queritur, ut tribūnīcia intercessiō armīs notārētur atque opprimerētur, quae superiōribus annīs armīs esset restitūta. Sullam nūdātā omnibus rēbus
10 tribūnīciā potestāte tamen intercessiōnem līberam relīquisse. Pompēium, quī āmissa restituisse videātur, dōna etiam, quae ante habuerint, adēmisse.... Hortātur, cūius imperātōris ductū VIIII annīs rem pūblicam fēlīcissimē gesserint plūrimaque proelia secunda
15 fēcerint, omnem Galliam Germāniamque pācāverint, ut ēius existimātiōnem dignitātemque ab inimīcīs dēfendant. Conclāmant legiōnis XIII, quae aderat, mīlitēs—hanc enim initiō tumultūs ēvocāverat, reliquae nōndum convēnerant—sēsē parātōs esse imperātōris suī
20 tribūnōrumque plēbis iniūriās dēfendere.

LESSON XX

Pompey and Labienus Abuse Their Victory over Caesar

Dē Bellō Cīvīlī 3.71

What Caesar Actually Wrote (p. 187)

[*DBC* 3.71] Duōbus hīs ūnīus diēī proeliīs Caesar dēsīderāvit mīlitēs DCCCCLX [nōnagentī quadrāgintā] et nōtōs equitēs Rōmānōs Tūticānum Gallum, senātōris fīlium, Gāium Fleginātem Placentiā, Aulum Grānium
5   Puteolīs, Marcum Sacrātivirum Capuā, tribūnōs mīlitum et centuriōnēs XXXII [trīgintā duo]; sed hōrum omnium pars magna in fossīs mūnītiōnibusque et flūminis rīpīs oppressa suōrum in terrōre ac fugā sine ullō vulnere interiit; signaque sunt mīlitāria amissa XXXII [trīgintā
10   duo]. Pompēius eō proeliō imperātor est appellātus. Hoc nōmen obtinuit atque ita sē posteā salūtārī passus est, sed neque in litterīs scrībere est solitus, neque in fascibus insignia laureae praetulit. At Labiēnus, cum ab eō impetrāvisset, ut sibi captīvōs trādī iubēret, omnēs
15   prōductōs ostentātiōnis, ut vidēbātur, causā, quō māior perfugae fidēs habērētur, commīlitōnēs appellāns et magnā verbōrum contumēliā interrogāns, solērentne veterānī mīlitēs fugere, in omnium conspectū interfēcit.

LESSON XXI

Pride before the Fall? The Pompeians Celebrate Their Victory

Dē Bellō Cīvīlī 3.72

What Caesar Actually Wrote (p. 197)

[*DBC* 3.72] Hīs rēbus tantum fīdūciae ac spīritūs
Pompēiānīs accessit, ut nōn dē ratiōne bellī cōgitārent,
sed vīcisse iam vidērentur. Nōn illī paucitātem nostrōrum
mīlitum, nōn inīquitātem locī atque angustiās
5   praeoccupātīs castrīs et ancipitem terrōrem intrā extrāque
mūnītiōnēs, nōn abscīsum in duās partēs exercitum, cum
altera alterī auxilium ferre nōn posset, causae fuisse
cōgitābant. Nōn ad haec addēbant nōn concursū ācrī
factō, nōn proeliō dīmicātum, sibique ipsōs multitūdine
10 atque angustiīs māius attulisse dētrīmentum, quam
ab hoste accēpissent. Nōn dēnique commūnēs bellī
cāsūs recordābantur, quam parvulae saepe causae vel
falsae suspīciōnis vel terrōris repentīnī vel obiectae
religiōnis magna dētrīmenta intulissent, quotiēns vel
15 ducis vitiō vel culpā tribūnī in exercitū esset offēnsum;
sed, proinde ac sī virtūte vīcissent, neque ulla commūtātiō
rērum posset accidere, per orbem terrārum fāmā ac litterīs
victōriam ēius diēī concelēbrābant.

LESSON XXII

Victory of Death: Labienus Insults Caesar and Swears an Oath

Dē Bellō Cīvīlī 3.87

What Caesar Actually Wrote (p. 209)

[DBC 3.87] Hunc Labiēnus excēpit et, cum Caesaris cōpiās despiceret, Pompēī cōnsilium summīs laudibus efferret, "nōlī," inquit, "existimāre, Pompēī, hunc esse exercitum, quī Galliam Germāniamque dēvīcerit. Omnibus interfuī
5 proeliīs neque temerē incognitam rem prōnūntiō. Perexigua pars illīus exercitūs superest; magna pars dēperiit, quod accidere tot proeliīs fuit necesse, multōs autumnī pestilentia in Ītaliā cōnsūmpsit, multī domum discessērunt, multī sunt relictī in continentī. An nōn
10 audistis ex eīs, quī per causam valētūdinis remānsērunt, cohortēs esse Brundisī factās? Hae cōpiae, quās vidētis, ex dīlectibus hōrum annōrum in citeriōre Galliā sunt refectae, et plērīque sunt ex colōniīs Trānspadānīs. Ac tamen quod fuit rōboris duōbus proeliīs Dyrrachīnīs
15 interiit." Haec cum dīxisset, iūrāvit sē nisi victōrem in castra nōn reversūrum reliquōsque, ut idem facerent, hortātus est. Hoc laudāns Pompēius idem iūrāvit; nec vērō ex reliquīs fuit quisquam, quī iūrāre dubitāret. Haec cum facta sunt in cōnsiliō, magnā spē et laetitiā omnium
20 discessum est; ac iam animō victōriam praecipiēbant, quod dē rē tantā et ā tam perītō imperātōre nihil frūstrā cōnfirmārī vidēbātur.

LESSON XXIII

Caesar Routes the Pompeians
Dē Bellō Cīvīlī 3.95

What Caesar Actually Wrote (p. 221)

[*DBC* 3.95] Caesar Pompēiānīs ex fugā intrā vallum compulsīs nullum spatium perterritīs darī oportēre existimans mīlitēs cohortātus est, ut beneficiō fortūnae ūterentur castraque oppugnārent. Quī, etsī magnō aestū
5 fatīgātī (nam ad merīdiem rēs erat perducta), tamen ad omnem labōrem animō parātī, imperiō pāruērunt. Castra ā cohortibus, quae ibi praesidiō erant relictae, industriē dēfendēbantur, multō etiam ācrius ā Thrācibus barbarīsque auxiliīs. Nam quī aciē refūgerant mīlitēs, et
10 animō perterritī et lassitūdine confectī, missīs plērīque armīs signīsque mīlitāribus, magīs dē reliquā fugā quam dē castrōrum dēfensiōne cōgitābant. Neque vērō diūtius [mīlitēs], quī in vallō constiterant, multitūdinem tēlōrum sustinēre potuērunt, sed confectī vulneribus
15 locum relīquērunt, prōtinusque omnēs ducibus ūsī centuriōnibus tribūnīsque mīlitum in altissimōs montēs, quī ad castra pertinēbant, confugērunt.

LESSON XXIV

Caesar Visits Pompey's Camp, but Pompey Escapes

Dē Bellō Cīvīlī 3.96

What Caesar Actually Wrote (p. 227)

[*DBC* 3.96] In castrīs Pompēī vidēre licuit trichilās structās, magnum argentī pondus expositum, recentibus caespitibus tabernācula constrāta, Lūciī etiam Lentulī et nōnnullōrum tabernācula prōtecta hederā, multaque
5   praetereā, quae nimiam luxuriam et victōriae fīdūciam dēsignārent, ut facile existimārī posset nihil eōs dē ēventū ēius diēī timuisse, quī nōn necessāriās conquīrerent voluptātēs. At hī miserrimō ac patientissimō exercituī Caesaris luxuriam obiciēbant, cuī semper omnia ad
10 necessārium ūsum dēfuissent. Pompēius, iam cum intrā vallum nostrī versārentur, equum nactus, dētractīs insignibus imperātōris, decumānā portā sē ex castrīs ēiēcit prōtinusque equō citātō Lārissam contendit. Neque ibi constitit, sed eādem celeritāte, paucōs suōs ex fugā
15 nactus, nocturnō itinere nōn intermissō, comitātū equitum XXX [trīginta] ad mare pervēnit nāvemque frūmentāriam conscendit, saepe, ut dīcēbātur, querēns tantum sē opīniōnem fefellisse, ut, ā quō genere hominum victōriam spērāsset, ab eō initiō fugae factō paene
20 prōditus vidērētur.

CONCLUSION & POST-READING

Valerius Maximus
Facta et Dicta Memorābilia 4.5.6

What Valerius Maximus Wrote about Caesar: A Modest Death (p. 235)

[*FDM* 4.5.6] Quam praecipuam in Gāiō quoque Caesare [verēcundiam] fuisse et saepenumerō appāruit et ultimus ēius diēs significāvit: complūribus enim parricīdārum violātus mucrōnibus inter ipsum illud tempus, quō
5   dīvīnus spīritus mortālī discernēbātur ā corpore, nē tribus quidem et vīgintī vulneribus quīn verēcundiae obsequerētur absterrērī potuit, sīquidem utrāque togam mānū dēmīsit, ut inferior pars corporis tēcta collāberētur. In hunc modum nōn hominēs exspīrant, sed dī
10 immortālēs sēdēs suās repetunt.

STUDENT TEXT ERRATA

The following errata are from the 2013 student edition of *Caesar: A LEGAMUS Transitional Reader.*

Page(s)	For	Read
vii, xv, 5, 9, 10	1.1–7	1.1
29	Add to Thinking about How Caesar Writes #1: Explain how this quote from Catullus connects to Caesar's narrative.	
37	Add to Thinking about How Caesar Writes: *ūnō*	
45	verb	word
48 #2	it modifies	each modifies
75	third sentence	fourth sentence
99	mood of verb	mood of the verb
	in that case	in that mood
108	tertiam	Tertiam
156 #5	Republican	republican
188 #4	How similar or different are they to each other?	How similar to or different from each other are they?

Macron Errors

28	bellans	bellāns
65	trānsire	transire
67	trānsire	transire
75	trāns	trans
216	*existimāns*	*existimāns*
217	existimans	existimāns
221	existimans	existimāns
123	Germānī	Germānī
229	Caesarīs	Caesaris

Made in the USA
San Bernardino, CA
24 May 2017